Healthy Eating

ISSUES
(formerly Issues for the Nineties)

Volume 36

Editor

Craig Donnellan

Independence
Educational Publishers
Cambridge

First published by Independence
PO Box 295
Cambridge CB1 3XP
England

British Library Cataloguing in Publication Data
Healthy Eating – (Issues Series)
I. Donnellan, Craig II. Series
641.3'0941

ISBN 1 86168 169 0

Printed in Great Britain
The Burlington Press
Cambridge

Typeset by
Claire Boyd

Cover
The illustration on the front cover is by
Pumpkin House.

CONTENTS

Introduction

Healthy Eating is the thirty-sixth volume in the **Issues** series. The aim of this series is to offer up-to-date information about important issues in our world.

Healthy Eating examines diet and food safety issues.

The information comes from a wide variety of sources and includes:
Government reports and statistics
Newspaper reports and features
Magazine articles and surveys
Literature from lobby groups
and charitable organisations.

It is hoped that, as you read about the many aspects of the issues explored in this book, you will critically evaluate the information presented. It is important that you decide whether you are being presented with facts or opinions. Does the writer give a biased or an unbiased report? If an opinion is being expressed, do you agree with the writer?

Healthy Eating offers a useful starting-point for those who need convenient access to information about the many issues involved. However, it is only a starting-point. At the back of the book is a list of organisations which you may want to contact for further information.

*****

Enjoy healthy eating

The balance of good health

In Britain our eating habits are changing all the time. There is now a much greater choice of foods available in our shops.

These include imported foods, which are a traditional part of eating patterns in other countries, as well as imaginative new ideas from food manufacturers. As a result, it has become more difficult to know which foods to choose, and how much of each, for a healthy diet.

This information will help you to choose a variety of foods so that you can eat healthily and enjoy it. It also explains how to prepare favourite foods in a healthier way, and explains about food additives and the labelling of foods.

Healthy eating helps reduce the risk of developing many conditions such as heart disease, cancer, constipation, obesity, and tooth decay. By eating a good variety and balance of foods, taking regular exercise, not drinking too much, and not smoking at all, you can give yourself the best chance of living a fitter and healthier life.

Don't be put off by the amount of advice given in this information – you don't have to follow it all. Try the suggestions that you would find easy and practical, that suit your lifestyle and that you can afford. You don't have to change all your eating habits at once. Start with one or two of the ideas suggested here, then introduce others gradually.

While the advice in this information applies to most people there are some exceptions. It does not apply to children under two years of age, about whom your health visitor, doctor or local health promotion unit can give you information. Between the ages of two and five, the eating patterns described here should be gradually introduced. Some elderly people and those under medical supervision may have special needs. Your doctor may refer you to a dietitian for advice.

The way to healthy eating

- Enjoy your food.
- Eat a variety of different foods.
- Eat plenty of foods rich in starch and fibre.
- Eat plenty of fruit and vegetables.
- Don't eat too many foods that contain a lot of fat.
- Don't have sugary foods and drinks too often.
- If you drink alcohol, drink sensibly.
- Eat the right amount to be a healthy weight.

Enjoy your food

Eating is an important part of everyone's life. Foods are chosen for all sorts of reasons, not just to get the nutrients you need. The taste, smell, colour, and how foods look are all important. Religion, cost, availability, and the way you live may all affect the choices you make about the foods you eat.

Eating may be a chance to sit down with the family or for a social occasion with friends. Or it may be a rushed snack grabbed during a spare five minutes.

Above all, it's important to enjoy food. To eat healthily you don't have to give up any of the foods you enjoy most. However, some foods should not be eaten too often or in large quantities if you want to be sure of enjoying good health.

Enjoy variety

Food provides nutrients to help the body work properly. A mixture of nutrients is obtained from food. No single food contains them all in the amounts needed, so we have to eat a mixture of foods to get the right amount. However, we need to eat more of some types of food than others.

The Balance of Good Health (shown overleaf) shows the types of foods and the proportions you need to eat them in to have a well-balanced, healthy diet. Foods that

are eaten as snacks and between meals count as well as food eaten at mealtimes. There are five different food groups. These are:

- Bread, other cereals and potatoes.
- Fruit and vegetables.
- Milk and dairy foods.
- Meat, fish and alternatives.
- Foods containing fat; foods containing sugar.

Try to eat some foods from the first four food groups every day. It is also important to vary the foods chosen from each group to get a mixture of all the different nutrients needed to maintain our health. Foods in the fifth group (foods containing fat; foods containing sugar) add variety to our diet but should not be eaten too often or in large amounts and should not replace foods from other groups.

The balance of good health

For most people the move towards a healthy balanced diet means eating more bread, breakfast cereals, potatoes, pasta and rice, and more fruit and vegetables. Above all we should aim for variety in our food.

Bread, other cereals and potatoes
This group includes:

- Bread, rolls, chapattis
- Breakfast cereals, oats
- Pasta, noodles
- Rice
- Potatoes, sweet potatoes
- Dishes made from maize, millet and cornmeal
- Plantains, green bananas
- Beans and lentils

Make these foods the main part of your meals. Eat all types and choose high fibre kinds whenever you can.

Fruit and vegetables
This group includes:

- All fresh, frozen and canned fruit and vegetables
- Salad vegetables
- Beans and lentils

Dried fruit and fruit juice can make up some of the choices from this group.

Try to eat at least five portions of fruit and vegetables each day. Include some vegetables, some salad and some fruit. Choose a wide variety.

Milk and dairy foods
This group includes:

- Milk*
- Cheese*
- Yoghurt*
- Fromage frais*

Meat, fish and alternatives
This group includes:

- Meat – beef, pork, bacon, lamb
- Meat products – sausages,* beefburgers,* meat pies
- Poultry – chicken, turkey
- Fish – fresh, frozen and canned
- Fish products – fish fingers, fish cakes
- Offal – liver, kidney
- Eggs
- Beans and lentils – baked beans, chickpeas, lentils
- Nuts and nut products such as peanut butter
- Textured vegetable protein and other meat alternatives

Choose a variety of foods from this group.

* Lower fat versions of these foods are available. Choose lower fat alternatives whenever you can.

Foods containing fat; foods containing sugar
This group includes foods we should use sparingly, like:

- Butter
- Margarine
- Low fat spreads
- Cooking oils
- Mayonnaise and oily salad dressings

And foods we can enjoy as treats, like:

- Biscuits
- Cakes
- Puddings
- Ice-cream
- Chocolate
- Sweets
- Crisps
- Sugar
- Sweetened drinks

Try not to eat these too often and when you do, have small amounts. Some foods such as beans and lentils fit into more than one group because of the mixture of nutrients they contain.

Eat a variety of different foods

Fat in food

This table shows the amount of fat there is in one serving of some foods, along with the fat content of some lower fat alternative choices.

Starchy foods	
Potatoes (140 g or 5 oz serving)	
thin-cut chips	17 g
thick-cut chips	8 g
oven chips	7 g
roast potatoes	8 g
baked potatoes	0.1 g
boiled potatoes	0.1 g
Rice (85 g or 3 oz raw weight)	
fried	8 g
boiled	1 g
Chapattis	
made with fat	8 g
made without fat	0.5 g
Dairy products	
Milk (284 ml or 1/2 pint)	
whole	11 g
semi-skimmed	5 g
skimmed	0.3 g
Cheese (60 g or 2 oz serving)	
Cheddar	20 g
Edam	14 g
low-fat cheddar	8 g
Cream (30 g or 1 oz serving)	
double cream	14 g
single cream	6 g
yoghurt (low fat plain)	0.3 g
fromage frais (low fat)	0.3 g
Fish	
Cod (85 g or 3 oz serving)	
fried in batter	9 g
poached	1 g
Fish fingers	
fried	11 g
grilled	6 g

Meat and meat products	
Pork chop (85 g or 3 oz serving)	
fried with fat left on	16 g
grilled with fat removed	6 g
Sausages (2 large)	
ordinary	21 g
'low fat'	9 g
Beefburgers, grilled (2)	
ordinary	18 g
'low fat'	11g
Poultry	
Roast chicken (85 g or 3 oz serving)	
skin left on	12 g
skin removed	5 g
Fat and oils	
Spreads (10 g or 1/2 oz serving)	
butter	8 g
margarine (all types)	8 g
low fat spread	4 g
ghee	10 g
oil (all types)	10 g
Sweet snacks	
small chocolate bar	15 g
halva	11 g
sevyiaan	7 g
burfi	5 g
2 digestive biscuits	6 g
Savoury snacks	
1 samosa	26 g
crisps (small bag)	
ordinary	9 g
'low fat'	7 g
peanuts (small bag)	12 g
Chinese pastry with bean filling	6 g

Don't eat too many foods that contain a lot of fat *Source: Crown Copyright*

Guidelines for a healthier diet

Information from the Institute of Food Research

Eat a wide variety of different foods

No food needs to be totally excluded from your diet – except occasionally for special medical reasons. Try to eat foods from each of the four main groups (starchy foods, dairy products, meat and fish, fruit and vegetables) each day and vary these over the week. If you don't eat meat and/or fish, pay particular attention to finding sensible alternatives.

Eat the right amount to be a healthy weight

Try to fill up on low fat foods or those with less calories, like starchy foods, fruit or vegetables.

Eat plenty of fruit and vegetables

Try to consume at least five portions of fruits and vegetables per day. Potatoes are a useful source of several essential nutrients but don't count them as one of your vegetable servings. Pile your plate with colour; the fruits and vegetables with coloured flesh appear to be important in the protective quality of these foods.

Eat plenty of foods rich in starch and fibre

Try to base most of your meals around foods that are rich in starch and fibre (bread, pasta, rice, breakfast cereals, potatoes, etc.). These are versatile and usually cheap. Go continental and serve bread with every meal. Increasing your intake of starchy foods will also lead to a reduction in your fat intake.

Try to limit fat intake

We must have some fat in our diets because they are needed to absorb fat soluble vitamins or are essential to our health. However, too much fat in the diet, along with other factors such as smoking and lack of exercise, increases the risk of a heart attack or stroke. In this country we eat much more fat than we need and the UK has one of the highest incidences of heart disease in the world.

- Choose low fat dairy products and lean cuts of meat. Try grilling or baking instead of frying or roasting, and don't add fat during cooking. If you do use a cooking fat, try one that is low in saturated fats. Remember that fat has twice as many calories as the same weight of carbohydrate or protein.
- Children under five are growing rapidly, so cutting down their fat intake too much may mean they won't be getting enough energy. Don't cut down on fat for children under two.

Choose fruit or bread rather than chocolate or sweets

Eating sugary foods is the main cause of tooth decay. Sugars contain calories and no other nutrients.

Look after the vitamins and minerals in your food

Store foods properly and eat them as fresh as possible. Overcooking vegetables and boiling them in too much water will destroy much of their nutritive value. Try steaming, pressure cooking or microwave cooking.

If you drink, keep within sensible limits

It is recommended that men should drink less than 21 units of alcohol a week, and women less than 14 (1 unit is half a pint of average beer or lager, a glass of wine or a pub measure of spirits). Make your drinks last longer by taking smaller sips or adding a mixer or mineral water. If you want to drink more try the low alcohol or alcohol free drinks now available.

Taste your food before adding salt

On average we eat about 13 grams (2 teaspoons) of salt a day, but we only need about 3 grams (1/2 teaspoon). Too much salt can lead to high blood pressure. Most of the salt is added during food manufacturing, so choose unsalted foods and don't add salt during cooking.

• Based on information from the Health Education Authority (HEA) and the World Health Organisation (WHO). Issued by the Institute of Food Research – see page 41 for their address details.

© *Institute of Food Research*

The plate of the nation

A report on the national diet. Consumers are eating twice as much fatty and sugary foods as they should. Most people want help to improve their diets. But Government attempts to help now seem doomed to die. Urgent action is clearly required.

The dream

The *Health of the Nation* White Paper, published in 1992, for the first time set out a strategy to promote public health. It set priorities and emphasised, in particular, the role that nutrition can play in coronary heart disease and strokes. It set specific nutritional targets, aimed at reducing the amount of fat we eat, especially saturated fats, and lowering the proportion of people who are obese.

The NTF – a panel of experts advising the Government – was set up to identify and co-ordinate an action plan to help bring about this substantial change in eating habits through education, encouragement and persuasion.

Its work was guided by the wider recommendations of the COMA Report on diet which advises that reductions in fat intake should be balanced by a corresponding increase in other areas: starchy foods such as bread, potatoes, rice and pasta along with more fruit and vegetables.

The NTF developed an action plan aimed at reducing the amount of fat we eat to lower the proportion of people who are obese.

In 1994 the NTF made its recommendations. It set out suggestions for improved information and education and called for businesses in the food chain, caterers and health professionals to work together to improve the national diet. The Department of Health commissioned a working group to come up with a simple pictorial guide 'The Balance of Good Health' plate symbol – based on the recommendations of the *Health of the Nation* White Paper.

The reality

Obesity is on the increase. The Government target was to reduce obesity in men by a quarter and women by a third by the year 2005. But since the *Health of the Nation* programme began, the number of obese people has grown. For example, the proportion of obese women has shot up from 12 per cent to 16 per cent since the *Health of the Nation* programme started. Figures like these prompted the Co-op to take a detailed look at the nation's diet to see what was going wrong.

Taylor Nelson AGB, on behalf of the Co-op, surveyed 11,000 people, from 4,200 households, to find out what they eat and drink day in day out. The purpose was to establish the actual 'Plate of the Nation' and to compare real eating habits with what the experts say we should be eating.

People were surveyed about everything they eat in the home. The Co-op's results show that families are eating almost double the amount of fatty and sugary foods recommended by COMA, with these foods accounting for a total of 18 per cent (by weight) of the nation's diet – as opposed to the 10 per cent urged by nutrition experts.

The Co-op's findings show that people are eating too little of the starch staples or fruit and vegetables. Bread, potatoes and other starchy foods make up 21 per cent of our diet – instead of the recommended 28 per cent – and fruit and vegetables stands at 24 per cent instead of 29. Milk and dairy foods are slightly under the level suggested by COMA, 19 per cent nationally, instead of 23 per cent.

But more disturbingly, Co-op findings reveal that youngsters currently eat nearly three times the amount of fatty and sugary food considered healthy by experts. Overall these foods make up nearly a third of the diet of 11- to 16-year-olds (28 per cent).

Children (11- to 16-year-olds) are eating too little milk and daily products (16 per cent compared to the experts' 23 per cent); bread, potatoes and other starchy foods (20 per cent compared to the required 28 per cent) and fruit and vegetables (19 per cent compared to 29 per cent).

The real diet of the nation

Fruit and vegetables 24%
Bread, other cereal and potatoes 21%
Milk and diary foods 19%
Meat, fish and alternatives 18%
Fatty and sugary foods 18%

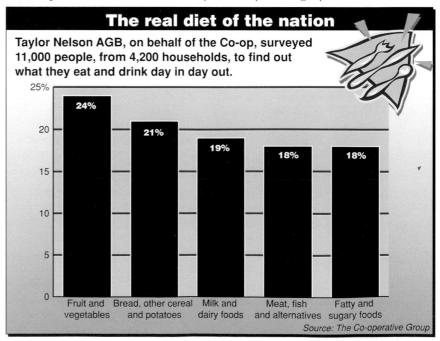

The real diet of the nation

Taylor Nelson AGB, on behalf of the Co-op, surveyed 11,000 people, from 4,200 households, to find out what they eat and drink day in day out.

Fruit and vegetables	24%
Bread, other cereal and potatoes	21%
Milk and dairy foods	19%
Meat, fish and alternatives	18%
Fatty and sugary foods	18%

Source: The Co-operative Group

The problems of balancing the family diet

The family study

Having discovered how far removed the nation's eating habits are from the Government's ideal, a further in-depth study was undertaken to find out why.

The Co-op wanted to look at the reasons why people have not changed their eating habits, the problems they have following the advice of experts and whether there are better ways to promote healthy eating in the population at large.

The researchers focused on meal planning and consumption and the findings highlight the everyday problems faced by ordinary families. Although small in scale the study allows a detailed look at the reality of trying to balance the family diet.

How was the research conducted?

Taylor Nelson AGB recruited 12 households, in different parts of the country. They completed two separate diet and health diaries to show the proportion of different foods eaten in the home.

The second diary was completed one month after the first, after families had been supplied with healthy eating literature.

All completed an in-depth interview – five of them after being accompanied on a regular shopping trip – as part of which they received an in-depth analysis of their own individual diets.

Another six households – which did not participate in the diary monitoring – were questioned by researchers. Two were accompanied on shopping trips.

Main findings

1. Attitudes to healthy eating

The researchers found a difference in attitude between families who consider themselves 'health conscious' and those who do not. The 'health conscious' had already got the message but need help to put it into action, while the 'non-health conscious' are not yet convinced that healthy eating matters.

2. Sources of information

Most of the families feel that retailers have a role in educating shoppers on healthy eating and some mistrust the Government. They get most of their health and dietary information from the media and with so many new nutritional theories being reported and then discredited, they are left confused.

3. Meal planning

Even for those already 'health conscious' there were a number of stumbling blocks which prevented them from eating as healthily as they might. Practical difficulties – such as the time, cost and hassle of eating healthily – were stressed. Only one out of our 18 families actually planned family meals in advance. For the rest, shortage of time to plan for meals means that many people eat the first thing that comes to hand. They may try to make it different to what they ate the day before, but that's about it. Speed, convenience and simpli-city, rather than health, are key to which foods end up being consumed in the home.

4. Feeding others

Most family members were keen to make changes when told they were eating unhealthily and when shown the balance of their own diets. But they all said the practicalities of trying to do so made this extremely difficult. In particular parents with children are under enormous pressure trying to reconcile the demands of the young ones with their own healthy eating beliefs. It's not easy to convince a difficult child to eat an apple instead of a bar of chocolate. Women tend to eat more healthily than men and see husbands as less ready to accept – let alone act on – healthy eating messages.

5. Changing behaviour

What was clear from most families taking part was that under normal circumstances it was unlikely they would change their diets. It was felt that for most people it would take a major event – a shock such as a heart attack, or pregnancy – before they would make a personal resolution to eat more healthily.

Responses to the Balance of Good Health Plate

Generally the Plate was well received by families – the proportions seemed to make sense. However on closer inspection some people found they didn't understand it as well as they had thought.

'The Plate is a quick way of telling you that you should eat a heck of a lot more fruit and vegetables than you should eat meat or fish.'

The Balance of Good Health Plate

Produced by the HEA:
Fruit and vegetables 33%
Bread, other cereal and potatoes 34%
Milk and dairy foods 15%
Meat, fish and alternatives 12%
Fatty and sugary foods 7%

'I always thought bread and potatoes were fattening, so I didn't tend to eat too much of them.'

The use of percentages is confusing for many – the popularity of dieting has led people to think mainly in terms of calories. They have additional mental blocks to overcome, having been brought up to think that bread and dairy products are fattening and that most people eat too much of them.

They also believe (correctly) that fish is healthy, and should figure as a greater proportion in a healthy diet than the Plate seems to show.

When their individual diets were compared with the Plate, most people found they were eating too much fatty and sugary foods and not enough fruit, vegetables and bread. Most people wanted to eat more healthily but still weren't sure how to do this.

Once people were told they had an unhealthy diet, most said they wanted help to understand healthy eating messages in down-to-earth, everyday language which they can understand easily – and act upon.

'I'm sitting here in a state of shock. I never realised what a bad diet we have. I am definitely going to start eating breakfast and grab a sandwich at lunch to redress the balance.'

• For further information about anything in this report or details of the survey write to:
The Co-operative Group
Freepost MR9 473.
Manchester M4 8BA

© The Co-operative Group

School children

A varied diet containing adequate energy and nutrients is essential for normal growth and development, which at times can be very rapid

Energy and nutrient requirements

The energy requirements of children increase rapidly because they are growing quickly and becoming more active. They have a high energy requirement for their size. To achieve this energy intake, foods which are high in energy (and also rich in nutrients) and eaten as part of small and frequent meals may be necessary for younger children, who do not have large enough stomachs to cope with big meals.

Despite this need for a high energy intake, however, it is thought that about 5-15% of children are overweight. These children should not be expected to lose large amounts of weight. They should be encouraged to remain at a constant weight or increase weight slowly while their height increases, so that they grow to be an acceptable weight for their height. Developing a healthy family lifestyle is important in the weight management of children.

A good supply of protein, calcium, iron and vitamins A and D is also necessary during this time. Calcium is needed for healthy tooth development and, together with vitamin D, helps make bones stronger. Childhood is an important time for tooth and bone development.

Children should be taught to think about dental hygiene and ways of preventing dental caries. They should be encouraged to reduce the number of times a day that they have foods and drinks containing sugar and, if possible, to have them only at meal times. Brushing teeth regularly with a fluoride toothpaste should also be encouraged.

Iron deficiency anaemia is associated with frequent infections, poor weight gain and delay in development. Iron rich foods, such as liver and red meat, are not generally popular with children, so other ways of providing this nutrient must be found, e.g. offering liver paté or minced meat hamburgers. Children who are vegetarian must have alternative sources of iron, such as dark green leafy vegetables, pulses and nuts. Other useful sources include bread and some fortified breakfast cereals. Iron from plant sources is less well absorbed than iron from animal sources. Consuming vitamin C rich foods or drinks with a meal can increase iron absorption from plant sources, e.g. offering fresh orange juice.

Healthy eating guidelines

Children over 5 years of age are beginning to take responsibility for their own food intake so it is important that they understand the need for a healthy diet. However, their eating habits will have been influenced by the family earlier in life, and it is difficult to change these once they are established. It is therefore important that the whole family has a healthy lifestyle.

School meals

School meals can make an important contribution to the energy and nutrient intake of children. They are thought to be the best option when compared with food brought from other sources such as cafés and take-aways, although there is considerable variation in the nutritional quality of school meals. The Education Act of 1980 removed the obligation for schools to provide meals of a set nutritional standard. However, voluntary nutritional guidelines are available for those who plan or prepare food available in schools, from tuck shops and vending machines as well as school lunches.

Some schools now offer parents guidance on the content of packed lunches, which are becoming more popular. This advice is offered as part of a 'whole school approach' to healthy eating through which the food consumed at school is in harmony with the principles of healthy eating taught in the classroom.

Children whose parents receive Income Support or Income-based Jobseeker's Allowance are eligible for free school meals.

School milk

Subsidised school milk can be made available to children in primary schools via the EC School Milk Subsidy Scheme. This scheme allows children to purchase 250ml of milk daily at a reduced price. Details of the scheme are available from the National Dairy Council.

© British Nutrition Foundation

Burger battles

School dinners may not mean boiled cabbage and pie but John Crace finds it is still a fight to get the little darlings to choose cauliflower cheese instead of chips

It's the calm before the storm. The cavernous, brightly-coloured hall of the Central Foundation boys' school echoes to the sound of food trays being laid out on the hot counter. In five minutes, the first of nearly 400 human locusts will swarm through the dining-room, munching their way through mountains of pizza, burgers and chips. Within 40 minutes the onslaught will be over and all that will be left for the caterers to do is decide how to dispose of the salads, the baked potatoes and the lamb noodles that will have remained virtually untouched.

School dinners have always come in for flak as few remember with affection the taste, or smell, of boiled cabbage and steak-and-gristle pie. But the debate has moved away from matters of taste to one of nutrition, amid fears that children are turning into junk-food addicts. Average sugar consumption has risen in Britain by more than 30% since 1980 and, according to the National Audit Office, Britain is the proud holder of the title for the fattest European nation, with 17% of men and 20% of women considered clinically obese.

Of more concern to schools is the alarming rise in obesity in children, confirmed by a recent report from the Medical Research Council. It concludes that today's children are more at risk of developing osteoporosis, heart and respiratory diseases and some forms of cancer than their more deprived parents and grandparents. Eating habits are learned primarily at home, but research by Mintel on behalf of Iceland has found most parents believe schools should be doing more to teach children about healthy eating.

But how do you convert that knowledge into practice? How do you get the little darlings to say no to chips? The simple answer is, you don't. You can put as many salads on

the menu as you like, but given a choice of eating healthily or bingeing on junk, most children will opt for the latter. Caterers dare not take junk off the menu because they know kids will vote with their feet and head for McDonald's.

There are no easy victories in the burger battle and most schools have reconciled themselves to a long war of attrition. Central Foundation is trying a different approach – stealth. Derek Powell, the deputy head, has been in charge of the school's catering makeover, involving a switch to new caterers. 'We have 840 pupils and only 300 or so were eating on site. Of these, roughly 250 were on free dinners. We looked at other schools and reckoned it was possible to get more boys in and make the food healthier and more appetising.'

So the doughnuts and pies have gone and a coat of paint, slicker service and a more appetising main course and pudding have come in. Powell has got it right on one count. Two weeks into the new regime and an extra hundred boys are using the dining-room, but they're nearly all packing in the saturated fats.

Jesse is first through the door, making straight for the pizza, burgers and chips. 'I always eat pizza,' he says, amazed that I should challenge him about his diet. Daniel and Bobby are on meal tickets, and for their £1.25 allowance they choose pizza and chips. 'You used to be able to get a drink as well, but they've put the prices up,' they chorus in outrage. So why not go for the main meal and pudding if you feel you're being ripped off? They look at me in disbelief, as the idea has clearly never crossed their mind. 'I need to feel filled up,' says Daniel.

The need to feel full is a common response among the boys when asked about their meal choice. But none associate feeling full with healthy eating. I only come across one boy who admits to thinking about his diet and eating salad. A couple have a go at the lamb noodles and cauliflower cheese and only one boy, Jake, opts for the ham sandwich. 'I actually wanted a slice of pizza, but they'd sold out,' he confesses.

Powell admits it's an uphill struggle to improve diets as there's a fine balance between a healthy menu and an empty dining-room, but he hopes to gradually ensure that chips are not a daily option. David Marney, senior operations manager for Chartwells, the caterers, appears unconvinced, but tries to reassure me that pizza is not that unhealthy before adding, 'we do make sure that the healthier options are the best value on the menu'.

But price is not really the issue. There is a certain correlation between low-income families and poor diet but these boys aren't stupid. They know what is and isn't healthy. They just don't give a damn one way or the other. They are still young enough to feel immortal, untouched by adult concerns of obesity and heart disease. In any case, they find the appeal and marketing of junk food specialists, McDonald's and KFC, infinitely more attractive than a few government directives.

Caterers dare not take junk off the menu because they know kids will vote with their feet and head for McDonald's

So what can be done? For the boys at secondary school the answer is almost certainly not very much – unless parents take more responsibility and stop expecting schools to deal with the problem in isolation. At primary school it may be a different matter. The department of social medicine at Bristol University, in conjunction with the health promotion division of the National Assembly for Wales, has been piloting a fruit tuck shop project in 28 schools in the west country.

'The aim is to get nine- and 10-year-olds to eat more healthily,' says Dr Joanna Moe, a researcher on the project. 'We targeted schools where there was no tuck shop, and asked them to set one up, to be run by the children, which only sold fruit. The idea was that if children had money that could only be spent on fruit, they would rather do that than not spend it all.' The results will not be available till later this year, but Dr Moe is happy with the results so far. But will these children take their good habits on to secondary school? 'Ah,' she sighs, 'that's the big unanswered question.' Watch this space.

Government launches free fruit in schools

Information from the Department of Health

A new Government initiative to provide free fruit to four- to six-year-old schoolchildren will be launched today by Public Health Minister Yvette Cooper.

The National School Fruit Scheme will entitle infant and nursery schoolchildren to a free piece of fruit each school day in an attempt to improve child health and nutrition. Children will receive apples, bananas, pears and satsumas as part of the scheme.

The first wave of pilot projects in London and the Midlands will be launched today and the scheme will be extended to hundreds of schools across the country from next spring. The NHS Plan states that every child in nursery and aged four to six years in infant schools will be entitled to a free piece of fruit each school day by 2004. It will be the biggest programme to support child nutrition since the introduction of free school milk in 1946.

Evidence from around the world shows that eating at least five portions of fruit and vegetables a day could lead to estimated reductions of up to 20 per cent in deaths from diseases such as heart disease, stroke and cancer. Experts suggest that it is the second most effective strategy in preventing cancer after reducing smoking. It can also help to prevent asthma – which now affects one in seven children – and respiratory illness.

Children, on average, eat just two portions of fruit and vegetables a day and one in five children eat no fruit in a week.* Evidence suggests that fruit and vegetable consumption has fallen in the last 20 years and that children growing up in disadvantaged families are about 50 per cent less likely to eat fruit and vegetables. These inequalities are reflected in health differences later in life; those in low income groups are more likely to suffer cancer and heart disease.

Minister for Public Health Yvette Cooper said:

'Every child deserves the best start in life. A healthy childhood provides the foundation for health later in life.

'But research shows that today too many children are not getting the healthy diet that could protect them against serious illnesses later in life – including cancer, heart disease and asthma.

'Like adults, children will make their own choices about what they eat, but too many people feel that a diet rich in fruit and vegetables is not a real option. For too many families, access to healthy food is limited, especially in some low income areas where affordable fruit and vegetables can be hard to find. These inequalities are reflected in health, as people on low income are three times more likely to die early from coronary heart disease than those from professional backgrounds.

'Children need the chance of a healthy start in life. That's why we are introducing free fruit for infant schoolchildren – to help protect them against serious disease and health inequalities later in life. For many children, this will mean a 50-100 per cent increase in the amount of fruit they eat.'

Hundreds of children in 35 schools in London and Leicester will receive their free school fruit this week. These pilot schemes will assess the best ways to distribute and promote the fruit to children before the next wave of schemes is launched in spring 2001 in hundreds of schools in Health Action Zones across England. In autumn 2001 it will be extended further across the country. The scheme is expected to cost up to £2m in the first year.

Minister for Schools Jacqui Smith said: 'Healthy lessons learned in school stay with children throughout their lives. The free fruit scheme complements DFEE initiatives. For example we will be introducing compulsory nutritional standards for school lunches – the first in 20 years – from April next year. Fruit and vegetables will have to be served every day as part of a school lunch.'

Food Standards Agency Deputy Chair, Suzi Leather said: 'The Food Standards Agency has a key role to play in the cross-government activity to improve the national diet. Young people are still not eating enough fruit and vegetables so it's great to see this scheme get up and running. By encouraging healthy eating habits at an early age we can really make a difference to their health.'

Food Industry Minister Joyce Quin said: 'This is good news, both for England's school pupils and for the UK horticulture industry. Encouraging people to eat more fruit should have great health benefits and will help towards meeting the recommendation of health experts of five portions of fruit and vegetables a day. It will also encourage a wider consumption of fresh produce.'

Notes:
* *The National Diet and Nutrition Survey*, which surveyed over 2000 4-18-year-olds, was published in June 2000. It found that:

- Compared to expert recommendations of at least five portions of fruit and vegetables a day, children eat on average two. By comparison, adults eat on average three portions.
- Children's consumption of fruit and vegetables has fallen since 1983. They were low in 1983, averaging about 3 portions a day. By the late 1990s, they were even lower, at only two portions a day.
- One in five children eat no fruit in a week
- Children in low income groups are 50 per cent less likely to eat fruit and vegetables
- Even those who eat fruit and vegetables eat less than one portion of each a day.

Diets of schoolchildren are heavily dependent on foods which

Children's consumption of fruit and vegetables has fallen since 1983. They were low in 1983, averaging about 3 portions a day. By the late 1990s, they were even lower, at only two portions a day

---

are rich in fat, sugar and salt. Nearly 70% of 2-12-year-olds consume biscuits, sweets or chocolate at least once a day. Boys eat, by weight, nearly twice as many biscuits than leafy green vegetables. Girls eat by weight more than twice as many sweets and chocolate than leafy green vegetables.

The first wave of schools to receive free fruit will be in three pilot health authorities. They are: Leicester, Hackney and Lambeth, Southwark and Lewisham.

Around 32 schools are taking part in the first wave this term. From spring 2001, hundreds of schools in Health Action Zones will become involved in the scheme and the initiative will be expanded further in the autumn of 2001

Many of the processes linked with cardiovascular disease begin in childhood and the early stages of cancer development start many years before there are any detectable signs

High intakes of fruit and vegetables are associated with a reduced risk of several common cancers, including colorectal and stomach cancers. Diets rich in fruit and vegetables have also been found to be protective against cardiovascular disease and respiratory illness, such as asthma and bronchitis

Ban the junk food ads

Crackdown call to curb children's danger diets

Television watchdogs face demands to ban advertising by brands such as McDonald's, Walker's crisps and Sunny Delight during children's schedules.

The Co-op warns that the advertising is threatening the health of youngsters by pushing products high in fat, salt or sugar.

It also accuses junk food firms and advertisers of effectively 'blackmailing' parents and using a number of cynical psychological ploys to hook children.

The Co-op backs up its attack with research showing that as much as 99 per cent of the food products advertised during children's viewing time is potentially unhealthy.

A further Co-op survey found three in four parents want a ban on campaigns which they feel blackmail them into buying.

The findings follow research by the Department of Health and the Food Standards Agency which exposed the appalling diet of many children and suggestions that Britain is on the brink of an obesity epidemic resulting from poor diet and a lack of exercise.

However, the Independent Television Commission is currently considering relaxing its code on advertising in a way which will make it easier for companies to target children.

The Co-op, which has pledged not to promote junk food products itself during children's schedules, wants tougher rules.

The ploys it identifies in a report published today include making products appear to be a child's friend, using animation, celebrities or heroes, and encouraging them to collect things and compete.

Advertisers appeal to the child's need for nurture and protection by associating products with 'goodness'. The sugary drink Sunny Delight is promoted in this way. They also appeal to the child's need for stimulation by

By Sean Poulter, Consumer Affairs Correspondent.

creating fantasy worlds. Using role models such as the Spice Girls to plug products is another trick.

Other brands, such as Domino's Pizza, are sold on the back of the child's need for peer group acceptance and a desire to be 'cool'. 'Our customers – parents in particular – are crying out for action to be taken against the mass advertising of these products to children,' said Wendy Wrigley, of the Co-op.

'Our findings clearly demonstrate the impact of food and drink advertising during children's TV viewing hours runs counter to the Government's healthy eating guidelines.'

The Co-op found that 73 per cent of youngsters said they asked parents to buy what they saw advertised.

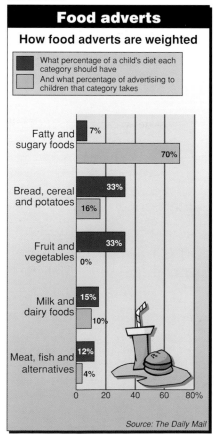

Food adverts

How food adverts are weighted

■ What percentage of a child's diet each category should have
□ And what percentage of advertising to children that category takes

Fatty and sugary foods	7% / 70%
Bread, cereal and potatoes	33% / 16%
Fruit and vegetables	33% / 0%
Milk and dairy foods	15% / 10%
Meat, fish and alternatives	12% / 4%

0   20   40   60   80%

Source: The Daily Mail

Some 51 per cent said they did not take no for an answer. Of parents, 77 per cent said they wanted to see a ban on adverts which 'blackmailed' them.

Separate research by NOP and Mintel showed which media characters, both on and off TV, have the greatest influence through so-called Pester Power.

Children of four and under said the Teletubbies and Winnie the Pooh were most likely to make them want a product. For children of between five and nine it was the Simpsons, followed by Rugrats.

The ITC proposes doing away with a rule that prevents the advertising of merchandise for two hours either side of a children's programme featuring the same characters. It says such ads should only be banned from the breaks immediately surrounding the programme.

Psychologist Dr Aric Sigman, who contributed to the Co-op study, said the adverts were 'crafted to exploit children's vulnerabilities at critical stages of their development'.

The research was carried out by Sustain, the food lobbying group. The most heavily plugged products included McDonald's, Cadbury's chocolate snacks, Haribo sweets, Kinder Surprise chocolate eggs, and biscuits such as Penguins and Viscount mint bars.

Researcher Sue Dibb said: 'This snapshot survey revealed a typical line-up of products which are high in fat, sugar or salt, all ingredients which the Government has identified as being a problem for children's health.'

The Advertising Association accused the Co-op of dressing up a marketing strategy as ethical trading and said: 'There is a huge raft of research to show that even very young children are able to be quite discriminatory.'

© The Daily Mail
July, 2000

The rich get thin, the poor get fat

Mary Killen knows why Britons are getting obese: because most of us, with the exception of a small elite, are tempted beyond endurance

The statistics that describe the problem of obesity in Britain, published today by the National Audit Office, are damning. In 1980, 8 per cent of women and 6 per cent of men were 'clinically obese'. Today, 32 per cent of women and 46 per cent of men are overweight or obese and, if these trends continue, one-quarter of us will be clinically obese by the year 2010.

One-third of Americans are clinically obese, a study published last week showed. British visitors to that country will not be surprised, considering the size of American helpings – cartwheel-sized pizzas, half-litre tubs of ice cream per person. Worse, these huge portions are becoming the norm here.

Remember when we were all satisfied with a small bag of crisps (25 grams)? They are hard to come by now, unless you buy a supermarket six-pack with 'fun-sized' contents. The new norm is 37.5gm.

Britons were once happy with 25gm bars of Kit Kat, Mars and Flake; now, king-sized bars jostle for dominance. A spokeswoman for Tesco says they sell as many as regular versions.

And yet, American calorific intake has decreased, on average, by 100 calories per day in the past 10 years. So greed alone cannot be to blame for the men-mountains seen wobbling through every American shopping mall, or carrying platefuls of bagels and waffles larger than their heads at every all-inclusive holiday resort in Florida.

Americans also tend to drive rather than walk, so a lack of exercise might be said to be built in to their lives. Add to this the fact that computers, DVDs and other sedentary entertainments are cheaper than ever and the tendency to bloat looks difficult to resist. We in Britain need to be watchful. Wittingly or otherwise, we often take our cues from America.

Temptation is at the root of our problems. Just as pornography corrupts people into performing sex acts that they would never have thought of alone, so we are titillated and tormented by gastro-porn shoved at us from every angle, which sets us slavering for things we were once perfectly happy to do without. We now think about food far more often than we used to. Television schedules are dominated by cooks, while newspapers and magazines seize upon stories about stars such as Kate Winslet and Sophie Dahl trying to lose weight.

Britons were once happy with 25gm bars of Kit Kat, Mars and Flake; now, king-sized bars jostle for dominance

---

Anyone watching *GMTV* will be agog each morning at Inch Loss Island, where volunteer fatties have been held virtual prisoners since January 15 to remove temptation and help them heed their dietitians' commands. So far, the experiment supports the theory that there is no such thing as an inability to lose weight because of a slow metabolism. Each volunteer has lost at least a stone.

Meanwhile, another production company is planning *The Big Diet*, in which inmates of a *Big Brother*-style house will be held captive and filmed round the clock. They will be selected for their inability to diet and will be tormented with tempting foodstuffs at all hours. The person who loses least weight each week gets chucked out.

The fact is that we think about food so much because it is all around us. Remember the days, perhaps as recently as 15 years ago, when an office worker would feel hungry at around 12.45pm and pop out for a not particularly enjoyable sandwich of sliced white bread, filled with ham, cheese, cucumber or tomato rings? She might have an apple and a bar of chocolate. Maximum intake: 700 calories. But she did not want any more. It cost around £2.20.

Today, we are assaulted by food pornography, even on our way to work, when cappuccinos, or ciabatta with American bacon, or smoked salmon and scrambled egg breakfasts offer themselves to us. At lunchtime, having chosen between sandwich outlets, we will be lucky if we can bring ourselves to leave with just our BLT – how can we resist a fruit smoothie, a low-fat carrot cake, a mocha cappucino or a bio yoghurt? After all, they are all 'healthy'. The cost could be about £7.50; more significantly, the calorific intake has soared. You can easily eat 1,500 calories just for lunch.

American society is pyramid-shaped – let us be careful our own does not become so. Throughout history, the rich have been fat and the poor thin. In the past 30 years, that has changed because there has been a revolution in education. The upper, middle and skilled working classes are interested in health and have learnt how to stay thin. But those who have remained immune to the information bombarded at them about the need for fibre and fresh fruit have continued to eat pasties and Mars bars.

Simple observation suggests that poorer, less educated people are more prone to obesity. Photographer Dafydd Jones, who has spent years covering social events in America for *Vanity Fair* and, latterly, *Talk* magazine, confirms it. 'All the elite in Manhattan are pencil thin. Not one of them is fat. The lower down the social scale you go in America, the fatter people are.'

The New York 'social X rays' have their own way of avoiding temptation. They have lunch in a restaurant that will allow them to order undressed mixed leaves – which take about 20 minutes of chewing but have no more than 200 calories.

At home they have a fridge full of processed cold meats, as *Skinny* magazine, an American publication devoted to the slimming tips of the rich and famous, reveals. An A6-sized slice of cold ham or beef takes about 90 seconds to eat if you chew it properly and 'costs' only 20 calories.

It's all very well for Ladies Who Lunch, but what about the rest of us who work, and are cold and hungry at lunchtime? The food sensitivity expert Gudrun Jonsson swears by her Thermos of organic chicken stock from Swaddles Green Farm. 'The stomach likes to have something warm in it. It helps the digestion,' she says.

'All the elite in Manhattan are pencil thin. Not one of them is fat. The lower down the social scale you go in America, the fatter people are'

Gudrun thinks the rise in obesity is linked to another digestive problem. 'Food was designed to be chewed. Saliva helps with the digestion. People today gobble food, and if they gobble fast food, it is worse. The food is not digested, the body still feels hungry. A quick fix can be had from a packet of crisps when it's a raw carrot that's needed. The blood sugar soars and dips all day.

'We are becoming a nation of foodaholics, like alcoholics. An alcoholic is fine if he does not touch a drink: if he has one, he does not stop. If we stay away from fast food, we are fine. If we have one beefburger, our blood sugar dip can only be cured by another beefburger.'

The relaxing of social inhibitions is another factor. Anne Wells, a debutante in the 1950s, remembers that 'in my day, it was social death not to be married and women were really well motivated to keep their figures until they had found a man and had children.

'I remember an aunt of mine saying to me after I had had my second child, "Well done darling, now you can let your figure go".'

Now most women don't need men for a meal ticket because they make their own money. The trouble is, the stress of doing so leaves them open to temptation. Enter the food pornographers.

Health drive targets beer and fast food lifestyle

By James Meikle, Health Correspondent

British males who live on beer and fast food – around a third of all men between 16 and 64 – are prime targets for a new government health promotion.

Analysis, funded by the Department of Health, of the diets of more than 2,000 men and women confirms that few young men breakfast on cereals, eat fish or shellfish, consume low-fat dairy products or drink fruit juice or wines. It is time such groups were helped to make healthier choices, suggests the team headed by Jane Pryer, of University College London.

'Factors such as convenience, cost, peer group pressure and occupation may be relevant to food choices and lifestyle,' she said.

Most men in what the researchers called the 'beer and convenience' category were under 30 and single. 'They eat a lot of fat and lack vitamins and minerals. Once you settle on a diet like this it can be a lifelong habit. Our recommended strategy would be to target health promotion at particular diet groups, rather than the whole population.'

The latest findings, published in the *Journal of Epidemiology and Community Health*, will come as a disappointment to nutritionists, even if they help explain why Britain has such high heart disease rates.

Most people studied by the researchers fell into one of four distinct diet 'clusters' which differed between the sexes. Less healthy diets were found mainly in the north of England and Scotland whereas those with healthier diets tended to live in southern, central and south-west England.

The beer and convenience category accounted for 34% of men's diets. A further 18% ate the 'traditional British diet' with high intakes of white bread, butter, tea, sugar and confectionery. A similar percentage (17.5%) ate plenty of fish, shellfish, fruit and nuts, and drank wine or spirits as part of a 'mixed, sweet diet', which also involved a lot of cakes and pastries. A further 17% had a healthier diet involving pasta, rice and coffee.

Among women, 32% ate plenty of white bread, butter and high-fat dairy products, but had low alcohol intakes. Nearly 25% ate a 'healthier cosmopolitan diet' with high consumption of whole grain cereals, low-fat dairy products, fish and wine, low intakes of chips and no beer or cider.

Diet and weight

Information from Mosby International

Why is a healthy weight important?

Achieving and maintaining a healthy weight is important for overall health. It can reduce the chances of developing serious diseases and conditions like heart disease, stroke, diabetes, high blood pressure, hip and knee damage, and constipation. It can also make you feel well and have more energy. To achieve a healthy weight and to stay that way may take some effort, but by sticking to the basics of a healthy diet, it can be done.

What is a healthy diet?

A healthy diet means eating a wide variety of foods from four main food groups:
* bread, other cereals and potatoes
* fruit and vegetables
* milk and dairy foods
* meat, fish and alternatives.

Bread, other cereals and potatoes

Choices from this food group should form the basis of your daily meals because they contain high levels of fibre and nutrients. Rice, pasta, noodles, lentils, bread and sweet potatoes are just a few of the options. When possible, choose whole-grain varieties as they provide more fibre, fill you up faster and help to keep your bowel movements regular.

Fruit and vegetables

Fruit and vegetables are an important source of dietary fibre and are rich in vitamins. You should try to include at least five servings of fresh, frozen or canned fruits and vegetables in your daily diet. Avoid overcooking as it can destroy many of the vitamins. Choose your fresh produce carefully. Remember that storing it improperly or storing it for too long reduces the vitamin content.

Milk and dairy foods

Dairy foods are a good source of protein and calcium, but they can be high in saturated fats. You should choose low-fat varieties of milk, yoghurt, cheese and fromage frais.

Meat, fish and alternatives

Meat, fish, poultry, eggs, beans, lentils and offal are some of the choices that provide important protein in your diet. It is a good idea to eat fish (particularly oily fish, like sardines or salmon) at least once a week, since these contain unsaturated fats. When you can, remove the fat from meat and the skin from poultry as this cuts down on the fat content considerably. So does the cooking method you use: rather than frying, try grilling, steaming, microwaving or baking.

Water

Water is vital to life. It is essential for the chemical processes in our cells and for the maintenance of normal bowel function. Try to drink at least eight cups of water each day.

How much fat can I have?

Although you should not eliminate fat completely from your diet, try to limit fat to no more than 30% of your daily calories. Use butter, margarines and oils sparingly – a scrape or a smear is sufficient. Cutting back on calories from fat leaves room to eat healthier foods, like whole-grains, fruits and vegetables – foods you can eat more of for fewer calories.

Some fat is better for you than others. Saturated fats (found in red meat and dairy products) tend to increase the amount of unwanted cholesterol in the body. Unsaturated fats (found in fish and vegetable oils) tend to decrease the amount of unwanted cholesterol in the body. You should therefore try to cut down on foods that contain saturated fats and eat more foods that contain unsaturated fats.

Should I avoid sugar?

Like fat, sugar is acceptable in small quantities, but overall it is not a vital part of healthy eating. Lots of

Eating habits

Respondents to the survey were asked about the food that they ate and the frequency of eating different types of food. The table below summarises the types of food ever eaten, eaten regularly and eaten occasionally. 'Regular' eating was defined as on at least two or three days per week and 'occasional' eating as about two or three times a month.

Types of food eaten	Ever (3153)	Regularly (3152)	Occasionally (3153)
Dairy products	96%	87%	5%
Fresh vegetable/salads/fruits	95%	86%	6%
Fresh chicken	86%	58%	23%
Eggs	86%	49%	28%
Other fresh meat	80%	50%	21%
Other conveneice foods, frozen or packaged (e.g. fish fingers, burgers, chips)	71%	32%	29%
Fresh fish	69%	29%	31%
Ready made meals (e.g. chicken curry)	56%	21%	26%
Organic food	34%	12%	14%
Any fresh meat	92%	76%	52%
Any convenience foods	81%	42%	45%
None	--	n	18%

Base: All repondents

Source: Consumer Attitudes to Food Standards, Food Standards Agency

foods, particularly prepared foods, already contain quantities of sugar. You may treat yourself with an indulgence (such as cake or biscuits) now and then, but make sure the serving is small.

How important are serving sizes?

Serving sizes are usually included on food labels to give an idea of the calorie and nutrient content. Serving sizes are one of the most important tools for a healthy diet, because they can help you work out if you are eating enough or too much food. Sometimes, however, serving sizes can be confusing and may be smaller than you think. This is particularly true for foods called 'reduced fat' or 'light' which may have smaller serving sizes than their regular counterparts. To make sure you know what is meant by a serving size, check the label carefully.

Can I skip meals to save calories?

Skipping meals may lead to overeating because you become so hungry that you snack on whatever is closest at hand. Make sure you eat regular meals and only occasional, healthy snacks. A wholesome breakfast should be at the top of a healthy

eating list, and it helps you stick to your eating plan throughout the day.

What about eating out?

Although you have less control over the ingredients and preparation, you can make healthy food choices even when eating out. Avoid fried food, especially deep-fried dishes, and ask for salad dressings and sauces on the side so you can control how much you use. Request that your meal be prepared in a low-fat way, such as grilling or baking. Portion sizes at restaurants are often larger than at home, so remember to leave extra food on your plate or ask that it be wrapped up to take with you.

What about drinking alcohol?

Alcoholic drinks are high in calories and offer no nutrition. If your aim is to lose weight, avoid alcohol for the time being, particularly because it can increase your appetite and

decrease your willpower. If you do drink, do so in moderation: two standard drinks per day for men and one standard drink per day for women is a good guide.

Is exercise important?

Exercise not only helps you lose weight or maintain a healthy weight, it also tones your muscles and helps you look more trim. Regular exercise is also good for your heart, bones and a sense of well-being. Try to be active every day by doing moderate exercise that you enjoy. Good choices include brisk walking, swimming and cycling.

How can I maintain a healthy weight permanently?

Achieving and maintaining a healthy weight requires a life long commitment to healthy eating. Learn to enjoy healthier, low-fat foods and realise that fad diets, liquid meals and diet pills are not the answer. Changing your behaviour is the key. Take time to assess your eating, cooking and shopping habits, and work out strategies to improve them for your long-term health and well-being. A good diet and regular exercise will help you achieve and maintain a healthy weight

Report on obesity

Information from the British Nutrition Foundation

The British Nutrition Foundation welcomes the publication of the NAO Report: *Tackling Obesity in England*. In common with other organisations, over the past few years the BNF has drawn attention to the many problems and public health issues associated with overweight and obesity, and the year-on-year increase in its prevalence in the UK and overseas.

Obesity is a serious chronic disease. Obese people are at a much increased risk of heart disease, stroke, diabetes, high blood pressure, some cancers, osteoarthritis of weight-bearing joints, gallstones, reproductive disorders, and complications

during and after pregnancy. Obesity also affects the quality of life of adults and children in many ways.

Obesity is a global public health issue. Although the actual rates are different the prevalence in other countries in Europe, North America and Australasia has also increased markedly over the last 20 years. Obesity is also beginning to be a significant public health problem in developing countries adding to the burdens of undernutrition, poverty and limited resources.

Obesity has a multifactorial aetiology. There are a number of contributory factors; the vast majority of them to do with lifestyle

and habits. The fundamental causes of obesity are sedentary lifestyles and the overconsumption of energy-dense diets. Very often in individuals or populations these two causes go hand in hand.

Obesity and overweight are the ultimate result of an individual storing energy as body fat because their habitual daily energy expenditure is less than their habitual daily energy intake over a long period of time. This could be because an individual, although eating an appropriate amount of energy and a balanced diet suitable for their age and sex, actually has a very sedentary lifestyle because of their job and/or leisure activities and/or domestic circumstances. Even if someone is quite active, they may still be eating more energy than they need because of the sorts of foods, and the overall diet that they eat.

The increase in obesity over the last 20 years has been paralleled by a decrease in physical activity. People are much more sedentary now, for example because of labour-saving devices at home and at work, using cars rather than walking or cycling even very short distances, and spending all their leisure time watching TV or playing computer games. In contrast the average amount of energy people eat has actually fallen over the same period of time, although meal patterns, and what, when and where we eat has changed.

Because of the many different factors involved, a holistic approach to the management, the treatment and the prevention of obesity and its co-morbidities is essential. The BNF therefore welcomes the identification in the NAO report of the importance of cross-governmental work between the Departments of Health; Education and Employment; Environment, Transport and the Regions; Culture, Media and Sport; and the Food Standards Agency. Any strategies to treat or prevent overweight and obesity should also build upon, and further encourage the development of, the many existing partnerships and initiatives between the food industry and retailers, scientists, health professionals, professional and voluntary bodies, the media, schools, and consumers.

Organic farming

The Soil Association

Organic farming is a way of producing food which recognises the essential connections between the soil, plants, animals and people. Organic food is ecologically produced which means that farmers use methods which mimic and enhance natural systems. For food to be sold as organic there is a legal requirement for it to be produced and handled according to a set of standards and each farm is independently inspected.

There is often a great diversity of farming operations on organic farms. This includes the growing of cereal crops, fruit and vegetables and rearing beef and dairy cattle, pigs, sheep, goats and poultry. Other activities such as growing hops, apples and vines for organic beer, cider and wine, or bee keeping (for honey), may also be part of an organic farm.

Fields tend to be smaller than those on conventional farms and boundaries such as hedges, ditches and dry stone walls are more obvious, giving the farm a more traditional landscape. Organic farmers strive to conserve natural resources and, in common with all farmers, to keep pollution to a minimum. The countryside and its wildlife are an integral part of an organic farming system and indeed the care of the natural environment is crucial if the farm is to operate successfully.

Consumer surveys have shown that more affluent supermarket shoppers are increasingly purchasing organic food. UK production of organic food cannot meet these demands on a regular basis and 70% of all organic food consumed in the UK is imported. Due to the increased labour costs involved in organic farming and other factors, produce is generally more expensive than that produced conventionally.

At present 0.3% of land in the UK is farmed organically by approximately 800 producers. By the millennium it is expected that the area of organic farm land will have risen to 1.5% and the number of producers will be about 3000. This increase is likely to be brought about by changes in agricultural policy and the provision of grants to those farmers wishing to convert to organic farming. The conversion period is up to 5 years and it is during this time that farmers need grants if they are to succeed. Once they are established, well-managed organic

farms, in some cases, can be more profitable than well-managed conventional farms. However, organic farms are unlikely to be able to meet the yields per hectare currently achieved by conventional farming.

Principles and practice in organic farming

The most valuable natural resource on an organic farm is soil and so it is not surprising that organic farmers place great emphasis on building up a healthy and fertile soil. Many organic farming methods involve this fundamental principle.

A healthy, fertile soil is rich in a huge variety of living things. Fungi and microbes help to rot and decompose dead plants and animals, recycling organic material back into the soil. Humus is that part of the soil made up of this partially decomposed plant and animal material. Organic farmers add composted manure and other farm wastes to soil in order to increase humus content which, in turn, ensures that more nutrients are available for plant growth. Such applications occur on some conventional farms, but often not to the same degree.

Crop rotations are an important component in most UK farming systems. Crops such as clover and grass improve soil structure and add nutrients. Others, like wheat and potatoes, take a lot of the goodness out of the soil. To 'rest' the soil and build up nutrients, farmers use rotations: growing a variety of crops in different places and at different times. Clover is especially helpful in building up soil fertility as it has special 'nodules' on the roots which contain bacteria. These bacteria are able to change nitrogen gas into nitrate (a chemical form of nitrogen that plants can use easily).

Animals are often involved in rotations as they can graze on the 'resting land' or ley, which would be sown with grass or clover. Sheep or pigs may feed on the root crops in a rotation and their manure feeds the soil and enriches it.

Organic farmers make best use of natural predator-prey relationships, rather than using chemical

---

There is often a great diversity of farming operations on organic farms. This includes the growing of cereal crops, fruit and vegetables and rearing beef and dairy cattle, pigs, sheep, goats and poultry

---

pesticides to destroy the flora and fauna that may damage a crop. For example, those insects that are beneficial include ladybirds and hoverfly larvae, which feed on aphids. Other predators, such as birds, bats, beetles, are encouraged by providing them with good habitats. This practice of rotating farm crops helps to break the life cycles of weeds and pests that may thrive if only one crop was grown over a large area of land.

Animal welfare

High standards of animal welfare are essential to organic farming. In all cases, animals provided with comfortable, clean shelter and plenty of space will be less stressed, more content and able to behave instinctively. Animals on organic farms are reared less intensively than on conventional farms, so are less likely to pick up diseases. On organic farms animals are outside in the natural light as much as possible. Pigs and sheep are moved to new ground regularly and this prevents a build up of parasites in the soil so the animals are, in turn, less susceptible to infestation.

Organically reared animals are fed a diet of organically grown food of plant origin. To comply with the regulations for feeding dairy cattle, for example, farmers must ensure that 90% of the cow's daily dry food is organically grown. The remaining 10% must come from specified sources and must not include any animal protein or genetically engineered products. Similar specifications exist for other farm animals.

Many organic farmers use homeopathic and herbal medicines successfully in the treatment of

disease, only resorting to vaccines and antibiotics when the situation demands and not as a matter of course. Growth hormones, used, in some countries (but illegal in the UK), to make animals grow faster, are not given to organically-reared animals.

Caring for the countryside and encouraging wildlife

It is in the interests of all farmers to care for the countryside and to encourage wildlife as much as possible. Keeping pollution to a minimum, conserving resources and providing wildlife habitats are all essential.

As chemical pesticides and fertilisers are not used on organic farms, toxins do not build up in the soil or in water where they might harm wildlife. Smaller fields are needed when crops are rotated and the hedges around them provide good wind breaks, helping to prevent soil erosion which can be a major problem on very large fields. Small units of land with more boundaries, such as hedges and dry stone walls, also provide valuable habitats for wildlife.

The Soil Association

The Soil Association is the leading UK charity campaigning for sustainable, organic farming and responsible forestry. 'Organic' is a term with legal status and all production of food intended for sale as organic must be inspected annually by an authorised body such as the Soil Association. The Soil Association logo is only awarded to food produced according to the rigorous standards required for organic certification. The consumer is guaranteed safe, nourishing food from healthy plants and animals, produced from a farming system where animal welfare and care of the environment are priorities.

• Further details of these resources, together with a Soil Association Mail Order Catalogue, can be obtained by writing to The Soil Association, Bristol House, 90 Victoria Street, Bristol, BS1 6DF. Telephone: 0117 9290661. Fax: 0117 9252504. E-mail: soilassoc@gn.apc.org

© The Soil Association

Are organic foods healthier than the alternatives?

Yes: Patrick Holden, The Soil Association. No: Julian Morris, Institute of Economic Affairs

Dear Julian,

Take the agriculture of a nation, subject it to 30 years of intensive farming, feed the resulting crops to consumers and wait to see what happens to public health. That is the 'experiment' being conducted in British agriculture.

On the likely outcome, opinion is sharply divided. In one camp are the vast majority of the conventional scientific community, the agricultural establishment and most of the cabinet. Their position has been 'You can't provide a scrap of evidence showing any significant differences between the quality of organic and intensively produced food. In fact all the indications are that public health has never been better.' But a growing percentage of the public feels that food grown without chemical fertilisers and pesticides must be healthier. This intuition is supported anecdotally by organic farmers convinced by observation of a direct link between the method of production and the health of crops and livestock.

Today at a conference entitled The Renaissance of Farming at the Royal Agricultural College, in Cirencester, Danish and German researchers will present new evidence suggesting that there are qualitative differences between organic and conventional foods derived directly from the method of primary production. In the light of this evidence surely even sceptics should acknowledge the urgent need for further research in this field?

Yours, Patrick Holden, Director, the Soil Association

Dear Patrick,

The only difference between 'organic' and conventional food is that organic food uses fewer synthetic chemicals. As a result, organic crops tend to have lower yields, so that more land must be used in their production for the same output and they are more expensive. To make up for this, organic farmers often use manure, which if improperly treated may contain high levels of the deadly bacterium E coli 0157:H7.

Organic food is also more likely to perish during transport and storage because of a reluctance to use preservatives. Many organic enthusiasts justify their reluctance to use synthetic chemicals on the now discredited grounds that they are carcinogenic. It is true that rodents given high doses of certain synthetic pesticides contract cancer. But the same is true for about half of all chemicals, including many found naturally in foods such as broccoli and oranges. We survive because the human immune system is able to deal with low doses of carcinogens.

Pesticide residues on food are not poisonous. The level of carcinogens from pesticides present in all the fruit and vegetables we consume in a year is approximately the same as the level of carcinogens in one cup of coffee. Fresh fruit and vegetables contain immune-boosting chemicals that enable us to fight cancer, so more cheap fresh fruit and vegetables improve our health regardless of the tiny amounts of pesticide residues that might remain.

Yours, Julian Morris, Institute of Economic Affairs, Editor, *Fearing Food* (Butterworth-Heinemann)

A growing percentage of the public feels that food grown without chemical fertilisers and pesticides must be healthier

---

Dear Julian,

I am surprised that your response manages to incorporate so many of the key misconceptions conventional scientists tend to make about organic farming. Your assertion that the only difference between organic and conventional food is the absence of synthetic chemicals misses the most important attribute of organic farming – that it promotes healthy plants and natural pest control.

An organically farmed world might mean a little more land in agricultural production. But don't forget that wildlife and biodiversity can co-exist with organic farming – not the case with high-input intensive monocropping. You also have it wrong on manures. Organic standards only permit the use of manures from animals on the organic holding or brought-in manure from extensive farming systems, both of which must be thoroughly composted before use, virtually eliminating the risk of any pathogenic bacteria in the crops.

The Environmental Protection Agency attributes 220,000 deaths a year to pesticide poisoning. Neither you nor I have any idea about what the long-term effect of consuming small traces of pesticides will be over decades, even in trace quantities. As for your last point, the latest research from Denmark suggests that organic production systems actually increase their presence, giving organic food stronger anti-cancer properties than its conventional equivalent.

Yours, Patrick

Dear Patrick,

Talk about misconceptions. First, organic farmers do engage in artificial stimulation of growth and chemical suppression of disease. They use copper sulphate and lime, a pesticide that kills indiscriminately, and they stimulate with shit, which contains an assortment of unpleasant chemicals. Is it good enough 'virtually' to eliminate bacteria through composting? And what about the 70% of organic food imported to the UK, much of it subject to less rigorous procedures than those of the Soil Association? Conventional farmers use a far broader array of chemical pesticides, many of which kill only a few target pests, and use fertilisers that target nutrient deficiencies without spreading disease.

Second, there is more biological diversity in a few acres of wilderness than in a million square miles of organic cropland. Third, nobody has ever died as a result of consuming pesticide residues on food, nor are they likely to. According to the World Health Organisation, over 90% of pesticide deaths are suicides; a further 7% are the result of household poisoning; the remaining few are the result of careless application. Many foods contain far higher levels of toxic natural pesticides than anything added by man.

Fourth, most studies have found no significant nutritional benefits from organic food; some have found the opposite. To adapt an old saying, 'manure in, manure out'.

Yours, Julian

Dear Julian,
Your depiction of organic farming as entailing crude 19th-century practices is a serious distortion of the principles and practices which govern it. Surely the challenge confronting agriculture is to develop systems which produce healthy food, using a minimum of non-renewable inputs and to do so without polluting, destroying wildlife, eroding soils or compromising food safety. Our contention is that organic farming is the best developed prescription which meets these objectives. The alternative is a brave new world of technologies with unquantifiable risks.

However, your points still need a rebuttal: copper sulphate will be phased out of organic standards by 2003; lime is not a pesticide but a means of neutralising soil acidity; animal manures have acquired their 'unhealthy' image largely because the

Most studies have found no significant nutritional benefits from organic food; some have found the opposite

bacteria and toxic residues they contain are the direct result of industrialised production; organic standards are remarkably consistent globally.

Your advocacy of target-killing and fertilisers and the separation of food production from the preservation of biodiversity epitomises the current 'food factories and parks' attitude that prevails in conventional science. This is the reverse of the organic philosophy. On your points about pesticide poisoning and food quality, we could trade further statistics on this but we have not yet had time to fully assess the effects of intensive farming on human health. What is beyond dispute is that more and more residues are finding a way into our food. Lady Eve Balfour, who founded the Soil Association in 1946, suggested that farmers should focus their attention on promoting what she called 'the causes of health'. She was right then and she still is today.

Yours, Patrick

Dear Patrick,
Organic farming is less healthy and less sustainable than conventional agriculture. In most developed countries, age-corrected rates of death from nearly all cancers have been falling for the past 40 years. This in spite of widespread use of synthetic pesticides and fertiliser. The simple explanation is that they increase output, reducing the cost of fresh fruit and vegetables, which help protect against cancer. Forty years should surely be long enough to show a causal relationship between pesticide and cancer if one existed; yet none has been shown. With our relatively high incomes, you and I can spend a little more on our sprouts and potatoes and buy 'organic' if we don't mind a bit of E coli, listeria, or aflatoxin. The vast majority, however, have no such luxury. For them, cheaper is better.

I'm glad you are phasing out copper sulphate. But I am worried that instead of permitting organic farmers to use better, more specific pesticides, you will force them to rely more heavily on carnivorous insects, which are more difficult to control. You will no doubt ban the use of such insects too. Unfortunately, such bans reduce the scope for farmers to develop better techniques aiming to combine the best of chemical and biological pest control. A move to organic farming is a move back to the days of our forebears when the masses had no choice but to eat the decaying and disease-ridden cast-offs of the elite.

Yours, Julian

Organic foods 'not more nutritious'

By James Meikle

The debate over the benefits of organic foods took a new twist yesterday after the government's food standards agency played down suggestions that they were healthier than conventionally grown alternatives.

Despite 40%-a-year increases in sales of organic produce, worth about £540m last year, the agency said there was no evidence to suggest it was safer or more nutritious. But claims that organic crops were more prone to toxins were disputed in a paper the agency described as 'balanced'.

The Soil Association, a standard-bearer for the organic movement, was disappointed by the agency paper.

Advocates of organics have argued that food grown without chemical fertilisers or pesticides must be healthier while critics have said they may be more risky because of naturally occurring infections and because of the liberal use of cow dung.

The agency said: 'There is not enough information available at present to be able to say that organic foods are significantly different in terms of their safety and nutritional content . . .

'A varied and balanced diet which includes plenty of fruit, vegetables and starchy foods should provide all the nutrients that a healthy individual requires, regardless of whether the individual components are produced by organic or conventional methods,' the report continued.

Comparisons had proved difficult in a government study into nutritional composition of organic and conventionally grown fruit and vegetables 10 years ago.

Research from Copenhagen University this year suggesting higher levels of nutrients in organic foods had only looked at one small component – polyphenols – in a few foods.

There was also insufficient evidence that organic produce was likely to cause more food poisoning. Most illnesses appeared to be caused by viruses which would not have originated from animal waste used as fertiliser.

Despite 40%-a-year increases in sales of organic produce, worth about £540m last year, the agency said there was no evidence to suggest it was safer or more nutritious

Similarly the idea that organics were more prone to toxins from mould had not been conclusively proved.

A spokesman for the agency said its stance might change as more information became available. 'Organic foods are a constant source of questions and worries so we felt we ought to put a position paper on our website.'

Harry Hadaway, of the Soil Association, said the agency should be seeking to join European research into the benefits of organics.

'We don't think it has taken into account the cumulative effects of a daily mixture of pesticides and veterinary medicines people are eating. The issue has not yet been adequately investigated scientifically,' he said.

© Guardian Newspapers Limited 2000

Soil Association responds to Food Standards Agency

The Soil Association is deeply concerned that Sir John Krebs of the Food Standards Agency is failing to inform himself and be objective in the ongoing national food debate.

Just yesterday Swiss scientists released a statement saying that they already have evidence that organically grown fruit and vegetables are healthier than conventionally grown produce. This supports other promising research already under way on nutritional value in Europe, for example in Denmark. A United Nations FAO report in July also concluded that organic practices can reduce e-coli infection that causes food poisoning and also reduce the levels of contaminants in foods.

Harry Hadaway, Soil Association spokesperson, says, 'A big problem in the UK is the lack of expenditure on research into the benefits of organic food. This should be a prime focus for the £20 million of tax payers' money that the Food Standards Agency was given for research.

'As a historic supporter of GM foods Sir John Krebs continues not to represent the wishes of the British consumer, who have made it clear that they reject chemical farming and GM food, due to the growing evidence of environmental and health impacts of this type of food production.'

The recently published *Biodiversity Benefits of Organic Farming* report proved, using 23 separate studies, that organic farming would significantly benefit wildlife in the UK. This report was supported and endorsed by WWF-UK.

© Soil Association

Antibiotics in food

Information from the Soil Association

62% of all antibiotics in the UK are used on animals

Antibiotics have been used as growth promoters in farming for nearly fifty years and their potentially disastrous effect on human health has only just started to be taken seriously. Most intensively reared farm animals in this country are fed antibiotics on a daily basis, as growth promoters, as a preventative measure or to treat illness.

Bacteria living in these animals can quickly become resistant to the antibiotics used to treat them. Antibiotics used in human medicine are often similar if not identical to antibiotics used in farming, and bacteria are able to transmit their resistant qualities to us very easily. The bacteria become resistant to the antibiotics we use to treat human illnesses, reducing the effectiveness of the treatment available.

Facts – use of antibiotics in farming

History

In 1953 the government passed a bill allowing the use of antibiotics as growth promoters in farming. This was following a post-war shortage of food and was welcomed as a device to increase production and reduce

costs. One side effect, which was not foreseen, was that the use of these antibiotics has a suppressing effect on disease. This led to 'super-intensification' which is the scenario we have on many farms today, with attractive savings for the farmer on labour, space and cost. The problem is self-perpetuating, when animals are kept intensively, they are much more susceptible to disease as they are being kept in unnatural circumstances, i.e. too many, too close together. This leads to increases in antibiotic use.

In the late 60s there was a worry when outbreaks of multi-drug resistant salmonella food poisoning were reported to be linked to the use of antibiotics in livestock production. The government set up an advisory body to examine the practice of feeding antibiotics to animals in relation to the issue of infectious drug resistance and introduced some measures relating to growth promoters, only to back-track over the next 20 or 30 years. Today use is higher than it has ever been.

Routine use of antibiotics in food products

Pork and bacon

On conventional farms, pigs are given antibiotics to promote growth and prevent the many diseases to which they are vulnerable when kept in close confinement and under stress. In total, pigs may be prescribed up to ten different antibiotics by injection, in water and in feed.

Chickens

Chickens destined for the table are routinely fed growth-promoting antibiotics used to treat parasitic infections. It is considered impractical to treat only the infected birds if a few fall ill as there is such a large number of birds in intensive systems, so treatment is given to all of them, whether necessary or not.

Eggs

Growth-promoting antibiotics are rarely used in battery hens, but the

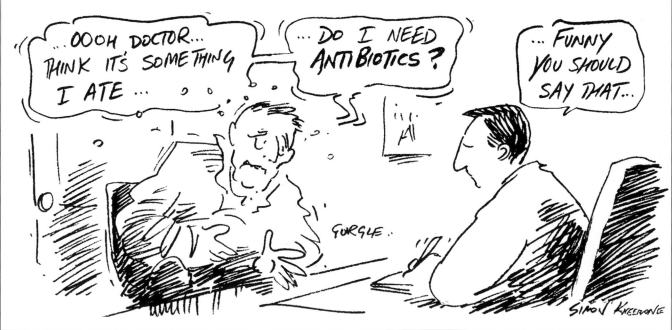

use of antibiotics to treat parasitic diseases such as coccdiosis can create residues. These residues have been found in up to 10 per cent of eggs. Intensive free-range birds and those in perchery systems are often given growth-promoting antibiotics routinely to control necrotic enteritis.

Beef

Intensively reared cattle are permitted several growth-promoting antibiotics in their feed.

Milk

In most dairy herds, cows have tubes of antibiotics inserted into the teats of the udder as a preventive measure against mastitis. This happens when they stop producing milk a few months before calving. Antibiotics are also used to treat diseases, including lameness which is estimated to affect 25% of dairy cattle each year because of high protein diets and poorly designed housing.

Fish

There is widespread usage of antibiotics in fish farming, even though it is recognised that fish absorb very little of the dose, and that most escapes into the environment. Residues have been found in wild fish, shellfish and crustaccans in close proximity to fish farms, and the concentrations can exceed levels accepted for human consumption.

Antibiotics in farming – impact on our health

Consumers are increasingly concerned about the impact antibiotic use in farming has on their health. The increasing use of these antibiotics can lead to bacterial resistance to the drug, rendering it useless when we use it to treat an infection.

Facts about bacteria

Bacteria are constantly changing in order to overcome adversity. They replicate by cell division, which means that the offspring bacteria contain the same genetic make-up as the parent cell. This also means that they can multiply incredibly quickly – in half an hour they can double their entire population. The resistant population will soon become the predominant popula-

tion, especially if the antibiotics are killing off the competition. These bacteria can easily transmit their resistant properties to our bacteria, either through eating food which is not properly cooked or from the environment. The problem is that as the antibiotics used in farming are similar to those used in our medicine, these antibiotics will not work on us when we are ill.

We all have millions of bacteria, most of which are beneficial and which we actually need. Two examples are staphylococci and enterococci. Staphylococci live in the nose and on the skin; enterococci live in the gut and both can live there quite harmlessly. At certain times however, they might end up in other parts of the body where they can become dangerous such as on open wounds. For example after an operation we are much more susceptible to infections in hospital as our immunities are lower and we are surrounded by illness. There will also be more antibiotic resistant bacteria present in the hospital as they can live in the environment as well as in people.

If one person in a house takes antibiotics for a short burst any bacteria which become resistant will soon become replaced with normal bacteria. If two people in the same house take antibiotics for the same period of time, it will take twice as long for the bacteria to return to normal. As this is the case, you can imagine the problem in hospitals where antibiotics are in constant use – the resistant bacteria will never have any opposition and the normal bacteria will not have the chance to be reinstated.

Food poisoning is another

concern in these cases – if we eat food which is not cooked properly for example, we may get food poisoning such as salmonella. If this meat contained antibiotic resistant bacteria, we would not be able to be treated by our antibiotics and could become seriously ill.

As these bacteria will be more inclined to work on vulnerable people, they tend to target certain areas more than others: in the hospital more than in the community, in intensive care more than in wards, in children and old people more than in adults.

Antibiotics in use

Farmers are now rapidly running out of antibiotics which can be used. The government has banned four antibiotics, which were previously used on a wide scale in farming. This may appear to be a victory, however farmers will only have one effective growth promoter left – AVILAMYCIN (marketed as Maxus G200). This is being pushed heavily by the drugs companies in light of this ban, the only problem is it is almost identical to an antibiotic being developed at the moment for human use called Ziracin (everninomycin). These two are completely cross-resistant and as Avilamycin is the only drug left farmers can use, it is likely to be used on an enormous scale.

MRSA is a term we now hear a lot, in fact we all contain MRSA (Methicillin Resistant Staphylococcus Aureus) and it is only a problem when it becomes an infection – there are now strains of MRSA resistant bacteria and these are on the increase.

We do have cause for concern; in 1997 the government banned a growth promoter called Avoparcin. This is almost identical to a human antibiotic called Vancomycin. Recently, Vancomycin resistant strains of MRSA were discovered in Glasgow Royal Infirmary. This is thought to be a result of the overuse of this drug in farming.

• The above information is from the Soil Association. See page 41 for address details.

A general introduction to food safety

Information from the Institute of Food Research

Introduction

Food offers an environment in which many types of bacteria can survive and even grow and reproduce. There are many opportunities during the production of food for bacteria to enter the food chain.

Chemicals in food can essentially be divided into two classes: those that are naturally present in food (e.g. natural toxicants) and those that find their way into food either through being deliberately added or through contamination.

Food safety on the farm

We need to minimise food-borne bacterial pathogens entering the meat food chain. Schemes in place include on-farm animal health, 'clean' livestock, and carcass treatments.

For example, the food-poisoning bacterium *Campylobacter* causes many thousands of cases of serious illness every year. Veterinary Laboratory Agency scientists recently focused on *Campylobacter* infection of poultry reared for meat on commercial farms. Changing boot dips twice weekly and changing boiler suits before entry into chicken houses, improving the cleaning of chicken houses between different flocks and daily sanitisation of feeding water all helped towards a 50% reduction in *Campylobacter* in young chickens.[1]

Microbiologists are concerned about the use of antibiotics as growth-promoters in some feedstocks, because of the risk that they may lead to the development of antibiotic-resistant strains of bacteria which may be transmitted to people. These are being reduced

By Catherine Reynolds, Head of Communications

and removed. Organisations like the Meat and Livestock Commission are actively pursuing effective alternatives to help growing animals maintain their resistance to disease.

What can producers do about bugs?

Major food producers, processors, distributors and retailers use Hazard Analysis and Critical Control Points (HACCP) to identify the microbiological hazards associated with specific food production processes, the points in the process at which the hazards can be most effectively controlled, and the means by which this control can be effected.

Natural toxicants

These are poisonous substances which occur naturally in a wide variety of foods. A few naturally occurring toxicants have been linked

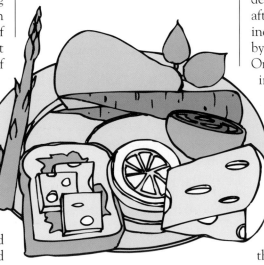

to harmful effects when foods containing very small quantities are eaten over a long period.

Compounds called glycoalkaloids are present at very low levels in potatoes; higher levels are found in green potatoes, sprouted potatoes or potatoes exposed to light. It is important that potatoes are grown 'earthed-up', so exposure to light is minimised, and stored in dark, cool, dry conditions whilst awaiting processing, at retail, and in the home. Aflatoxins are a group of toxicants formed by moulds in improperly stored nuts, grain etc. By limiting the levels of aflatoxins in animal feeds, the levels in milk and milk products are also minimised. Mouldy or damaged apples may contain a mycotoxin called patulin. Which is why processors have been advised NOT to use mouldy apples in juice production.

Pesticides

Pesticides are widely used all over the world. In agriculture they have helped to increase yields and protect crops both in developed and developing countries. They are used after a crop has been harvested to increase storage life, improve hygiene by killing flies and cockroaches etc. Only approved pesticides can be used in the UK. And only for their specific approved purpose – with limits on the amount that can be used on a crop, the stages of development at which it can be applied and the harvest interval.

75% of the agricultural pesticides used in the UK are herbicides, and many uses of herbicides leave no residues in the food. Maximum Residues Levels have been set down in law to control pesticides which can leave residues in meat and dairy products, cereals, and fruit and vegetables.[2]

The Government runs an extensive surveillance programme to make sure that crops and foods contain residues of farm chemicals which do not exceed the MRLs.

BSE

The safety precautions in place in the UK food chain are designed to minimise any potential risk from Bovine Spongiform Encephalopathy. Feeding cattle (or any other farm animal) with material that includes processed body parts of cattle and sheep is now illegal in the UK. Only cattle under 30 months old can be used for food.

> *If each product is logged from plough to plate, including characteristics of the product and everything that happens to it, then consumers are assured of the quality the product they purchase*

Traceability

Growers and processors must satisfy the agronomic and traceability demands of customers. If each product is logged from plough to plate, including characteristics of the product and everything that happens to it, then consumers are assured of the quality of the product they purchase. If an issue arises, then retailers can trace the suspect material through the food chain and isolate items quickly and effectively.

References
1 *Food Research News* Issue 4, 1998
2 *Pesticides Safety Directorate, Information Section* – e-mail p.s.d.information@psd.maff.gsi.gov.uk or telephone number 01904 455775.

If you have access to the Internet visit www.pesticides.gov.uk or www.foodstandards.gov.uk for more information.

Low public trust in food safety

By James Meikle, Health Correspondent

Five million people in Britain could have suffered food poisoning last year, but few reported it to a doctor or a food outlet that may have been responsible, the food standards agency reveals today.

Its survey of attitudes to food safety has found confidence to be 'unacceptably low', with less than half the population happy with the present regime, a finding that is sure to prompt a blitz on industry standards.

Three in five people were still worried about BSE, despite a rise in beef consumption, and about food poisoning in general. Concern was widespread about the way abattoirs and butchers handled raw chicken and beef, as well as hygiene in fast food outlets, markets and supermarkets.

Interviews with 3,153 Britons in October suggest that levels of food poisoning may be 50 times as high as official figures suggest, although the agency emphasised they reflected individuals' perception of the problem. But officials were concerned by 14% of those questioned in England who said they had experienced vomiting or diarrhoea due to poisoning. Fewer Scots (13%), Welsh (11%) and Northern Irish (10%) reported such incidents. Only 3% of people over 65 suffered such an attack while 20% of those aged 26-35 thought they had been struck down. Just one in five consumers reported their experience to anyone, and they were far more likely to tell their GP than the place where they bought or consumed the food which may have been responsible.

The survey found 48% were

> *The survey of attitudes to food safety has found confidence to be 'unacceptably low', with less than half the population happy with the present regime*

confident about safety measures. Sir John Krebs, chairman of the food standards agency, said: 'It may be a reflection of two decades of food crises, but it is an unacceptably low figure.'

Urban consumers were more concerned about food issues than those in the countryside, but they were also more likely to have suffered food poisoning. In all 63% of people said they were worried about food poisoning, 61% about BSE, while 43% had concerns over GM foods and 37% were worried by the level of antibiotics that might be present in the farm animals they ate.

The survey suggested that healthy eating messages from the government still had some way to go. Of the 43% who were aware of official advice to eat at least five portions of fruit and vegetables a day, only half did so the day before they were interviewed. Few actually knew what a portion size was – a whole fruit if eaten raw or two tablespoons of vegetable.

A third of those questioned had eaten organic food but just one in 20 households included a vegetarian.

Consumer attitudes to food standards

Information from the Food Standards Agency

The objective of this report is to help the Food Standards Agency improve its knowledge and understanding of consumer attitudes to food safety and food standards, to develop effective communication strategies and to gauge public confidence in food safety arrangements. *Consumer attitudes to food standards* surveyed over 3,100 people in the UK between October and December 2000, just six months after the Agency was created.

Food safety and hygiene

- Food safety is considered a key issue by most interviewees, though less so in Northern Ireland.
- Three-quarters of the UK population say they are fairly or very concerned about food safety. More than two-thirds (69%) are particularly concerned about the safety of raw meat. More people are concerned about raw chicken (54 per cent) than raw beef (53% per cent).
- Less than half (48%) were confident about current food safety measures.
- Nearly half of those surveyed thought food safety had improved over the last year.
- However, 78 per cent worry about food hygiene in one or more locations: meat stalls in markets (56 per cent), butchers (25 per cent), supermarkets (21 per cent) and the home (19 per cent).
- At home, 40 per cent have a fridge thermometer and 39 per cent claim to know the right temperature for their fridge (1-5°C), but only 61 per cent of the latter were correct and they tended to be in younger age groups.

Food-borne disease and responses to it

- Incidences of vomiting or diarrhoea believed to be from food poisoning in the past year were: England 14 per cent, Scotland 13 per cent, Wales 11 per cent and Northern Ireland 10 per cent. The oldest (66+) age group was less likely than any other to have suffered this problem. Over 80% of individuals who had suffered from a food-borne illness did not report it to anyone, and of those who did, most informed their GP and not the suspect food outlet.

Food labelling

- 59 per cent regularly check food labelling and of these 67 per cent focused on the best before/use by date, with cooking and storage instructions the next most scrutinised (46 per cent). 25 per cent found food labelling 'difficult to understand'. A third of this group were in the 50-65 and 66+ age groups. Only a third knew what to do with products that had either exceeded a best-before date or a use-by date.
- Comprehension of what was a significant level of fat, sugar and, in particular, salt, was variable and general understanding of ingredient labelling was poor.

Healthy eating and nutrition

- 55 per cent have not changed their eating habits over the past year, but 38 per cent said that their diet had become healthier. In addition, most are aware that they should eat more fruit,

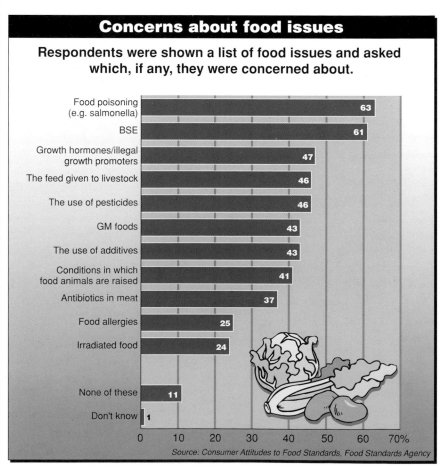

Concerns about food issues

Respondents were shown a list of food issues and asked which, if any, they were concerned about.

Issue	Per cent
Food poisoning (e.g. salmonella)	63
BSE	61
Growth hormones/illegal growth promoters	47
The feed given to livestock	46
The use of pesticides	46
GM foods	43
The use of additives	43
Conditions in which food animals are raised	41
Antibiotics in meat	37
Food allergies	25
Irradiated food	24
None of these	11
Don't know	1

Source: Consumer Attitudes to Food Standards, Food Standards Agency

vegetables and salad and cut down on fatty foods and sugary foods/drink although they are unsure about the benefits of bread and cereals.

- Of the 43 per cent who were aware of the advice to eat at least five portions of fruit and vegetables a day only half actually did so the previous day.
- Only 36 per cent are aware of the recommended daily intake of fruit and vegetables (five a day). The majority also have an inaccurate idea of the recommended portion sizes.

Eating habits

- 80 per cent eat staple foods – dairy products; vegetables, salads and fruit; eggs and fresh meat. However, only two-thirds eat fresh fish. 90 per cent eat fresh meat – with chicken being the favourite.
- 5 per cent of households include a vegetarian and 7 per cent include someone who is mainly vegetarian. A third of those surveyed claimed to have eaten organic food.
- 80 per cent eat some convenience food with frozen or packaged foods more popular than ready-made meals.
- 'Takeaways' such as fish and chip shops, Chinese, Indian and pizza places have been used by two-thirds of interviewees. Just under half also use restaurants and fast food chains.
- Hygiene in such outlets worries nearly 50 per cent of those interviewed, particularly in Northern Ireland, but this did not always mean that they avoided these premises. Those with less disposable income – for example those aged 66+ or DE social group – use all such outlets least, while fast food outlets are most used by the 16-35s.

Shopping habits

- Just over half of the interviewees take full responsibility for household food/grocery shopping, and out of these most are likely to be women (79 per cent). 94 per cent buy the majority of their food from supermarkets with local

---

Consumers commonly felt that they were given too little information towards making decisions about what they ate

---

shops favoured by the 66+ age group.

- Less than 1 per cent shop online.
- Less than a quarter interviewed usually buy food only for themselves – most buy for a household with a partner or children.

Information sources/ responsibility for food standards

- More than a third of people were unaware of where to find informa-

tion on food safety and the remainder quoted a variety of national and local government, media and commercial bodies. Of sources used, the media dominated with supermarkets following. Nearly 50 per cent thought it was the Agency's job to set food standards, but only a quarter believed it also enforced standards – comprehension of which bodies should carry out these roles was generally poor.

- Consumers commonly felt that they were given too little information towards making decisions about what they ate. Of those that had received information from the Food Standards Agency, 75% felt that the information or advice given was very/fairly reliable

---

Top ten facts and figures

Information from the UK Food Standards Agency Survey 2001

- 14 per cent of UK respondents have had at least one case of food poisoning over the last year but only 20 per cent of sufferers reported it. Incidences of vomiting or diarrhoea from food poisoning were highest in England (14 per cent), although country variations were minimal (Scotland 13 per cent, Wales 11 per cent and Northern Ireland 10 per cent). The oldest (66+) age group suffered least.
- 90 per cent of respondents eat fresh meat on a regular basis.
- 69 per cent of people see raw meat as a food health risk, with food poisoning being the most feared consequence.
- However, only 5 per cent of households include a vegetarian.
- Although most people think food safety has improved over the last year, 78 per cent worry about food hygiene in a variety of locations. These were: meat stalls in markets (56 per cent), butchers (25 per cent), supermarkets (21 per cent) and the home (19 per cent).
- Despite concern about hygiene standards in takeaways and fast-food outlets, two-thirds of people in the UK visit them on an occasional or regular basis.
- Although people know they should eat more healthily, many don't understand heatlhy food messages. Only 36 per cent of respondents know to eat 5 portions of fruit and vegetables a day for a healthy diet, and most respondents could not explain how to measure a 'portion'.
- Although 59 per cent of respondents claim to always or usually refer to food labels, understanding of the information on labels is minimal (25 per cent find food labels 'difficult to understand').
- Although 67 per cent of consumers who check labels said they were most likely to look at the 'best before/use by' date, only a third of respondents correctly identified what should be done with food one day past each of these dates.
- 94 per cent of shoppers buy mostly from supermarkets, with less than 1 per cent shopping for food on the Internet. 79 per cent of those responsible for the regular family shop are women.

- 43 per cent were fairly confident about food safety measures and 5 per cent were 'very confident'.

Awareness of the Food Standards Agency

- 58 per cent claim to have heard of the Agency and 32 per cent of these believe its duty is the regulation of food labelling. Informing the public on food standards and safety (25 per cent) is the other major role that is widely recognised. 52 per cent view the Agency positively with 21 per cent viewing it as negative. 32 per cent view the Agency as independent, while others think it reflects the views of other bodies: the Government (22 per cent), food industry (17 per cent) or consumer groups (13 per cent).

Whether the Food Standards Agency should Intervene

- 90 per cent thought the Agency should intervene on issues within its remit. Consumers expressed a desire for more information on food safety, including fundamentals such as hygiene, storage and labelling. 39 per cent also wanted more information about the Agency. 25 per cent recall seeing information about the Agency, including press and TV reports.

Differences within the UK

Northern Ireland:

- The greatest concern was about hygiene in takeaway, mobile and fast-food outlets.
- In Northern Ireland consumers claimed to have the lowest proportion of daily vegetable consumption.
- There were consistently lower levels of concern about food safety issues and they had the least awareness of where to go for food safety and standards information. There was a lower awareness of the Agency and its role in general.

Scotland:

- Most were aware of the Agency and of its role as an information source and most were likely to see the Agency as independent and unbiased.

- Scotland remains a nation of meat eaters (96 per cent) with chicken the favourite choice.

Wales and England:

- Consumers in England had a significantly higher claimed frequency of checking food labels compared with Northern Ireland and Wales.
- The survey reveals Wales as a nation where women (83 per cent) are still the main shoppers of the household and 95 per cent of people prefer to buy most groceries from the supermarket.
- 11% of interviewees in Wales claimed to have suffered vomiting or diarrhoea from food poisoning during the past year.

Population groups:

- Urban consumers were more concerned about food issues and reported that they had suffered higher levels of food poisoning during the past year than rural consumers.

Age groups:

- The 16-25s were least likely to be responsible for food shopping and were highly fast-food orientated. The 66+ group were least likely to eat out and were most likely to use local shops and buy food only for themselves.
- On some measures there was progression across the age groups. For example, difficulty with understanding labels increased with age though the youngest and oldest age groups (16-25s and 66+) were the least concerned about food labelling accuracy and the least aware of the Agency.
- The 66+ group was least concerned about food safety and notably about outlet hygiene, specific foods or food issues. They were also least likely to have suffered food poisoning or to adopt a healthier diet. They perhaps felt it was too late to change habits and that food safety was better now than when they were young, but this promoted a risk that they might 'tune out' important food safety messages.

Social groups:

- ABs were more likely to be concerned and seek information across all issues, while DEs tended to be least concerned – concern amongst C1C2s varied between both extremes. ABs tended to be better informed about some issues such as recommended daily portions and checking levels of fat and sugar, and more were trying to eat more healthily. ABs were also more aware of the Agency and its roles.

- The above information is from the executive summary of the Food Standards Agency's report *Consumer Attitudes to Food Standards*.

Tackling BSE

European Union agriculture ministers agree to incinerate any cow over 30 months old that has not tested negative for BSE

After a stormy late-night session in Brussels, European Union agriculture ministers have agreed new measures to fight the spread of mad cow disease.

All countries in the EU will incinerate any cow over 30 months old that has not tested negative for BSE. It will also ban nearly all animal remains in feed for all livestock. Both measures came into force in January 2001.

The dramatic decision to destroy any untested cow over 30 months old means, in practice, that all older cattle in the EU will be incinerated rather than eaten until well into 2001. This is because fast BSE testing is unlikely to be available in all abattoirs across the EU for at least another six months.

The impact will be immense, to judge from the experience of Britain. It banned the consumption of cattle over 30 months old in 1996, when BSE was linked to the human disease vCJD. BSE is thought to become detectable, and infectious, at 30 months.

Burning beef mountain

More than 4.6 million older British dairy cows have been slaughtered and rendered so far, leaving 613,000 tonnes of tallow and meat and bone meal. Britain only started incinerating the mountain of remains this year. It will take until 2004 to burn the backlog.

The rest of the EU could pile up a similar mountain before testing is available. The European Commission will pay 70 per cent of the costs. But Europe is still searching for sufficient incinerators. Most countries expect to use cement plants.

All countries in the EU will incinerate any cow over 30 months old that has not tested negative for BSE. It will also ban nearly all animal remains in feed for all livestock

---

Countries that have not yet reported any cases of BSE want an exemption from the measures. They are thought to include Sweden, Finland and Austria. The Commission has promised to study 'whether an exception is acceptable'.

But scientists advising the Commission say privately that they want wide-ranging tests to determine the true incidence of BSE in all EU countries, before anyone is let off the hook.

Protein and fat

The second major measure adopted is a feed ban. Currently, all EU countries except the UK feed meat and bone meal (MBM) from slaughtered animals, including cattle, to pigs, chickens and fish. This will now be forbidden for six months, while experts determine whether contamination of cattle feed with MBM was responsible for spreading BSE.

It will be hard for farmers to replace MBM in feed, especially for pigs. The Commission is studying ways to boost Europe's production of high-protein legume plants, which is limited under international trade agreements.

The fat in rendered animal remains will be even harder to replace, as plant oils do not contain the required fatty acids. Despite objections from Germany, the ministers decided pigs and chickens may still eat fat rendered from slaughtered animals.

• From *New Scientist*, 5 December 2000

From farm to plate

A sick industry

The drive for agricultural efficiency has produced high yields and low prices – but the benefits have come at a price

- Farming has become increasingly intensive, large scale and globalised in the drive for cheaper food
- In the last 10 years in Britain, the number of farms has fallen 25%, to 168,000 from 233,000
- Animals are reared on production lines. About 750m broiler chickens are reared and slaughtered in Britain each year, 98% of them intensively. They spend the last week of their lives in a space the size of an A4 sheet of paper. The spread of disease is a problem
- In two decades, new production methods have increased a dairy cow's average yield from 4,000 litres to 5,800 litres a year
- A cow named Marissa is set to break milk records: at nine years old, she had produced more than 100,000 litres of milk from just seven calvings, averaging 35 litres a day for 10 years
- In 2000, 939,000 tonnes of pork and bacon were produced in Britain, 210,000 tonnes were exported and 520,000 imported
- Food processors usually want large quantities of uniform quality produce or animals at specific times. This is ideally suited to intensive farming methods which favour synthetic chemicals, land degradation and animal welfare problems
- Processed food may be of high nutritional quality, but it can add to environmental and social costs
- Often, food must be taken long distances to factories. Animal welfare groups have long fought to improve the conditions of animals which are routinely moved hundreds of miles in cramped conditions

Farming has become increasingly intensive, large scale and globalised in the drive for cheaper food

- Because people buy so much in the way of processed ready meals, they often do not understand the need for proper cooking. This leads to greater potential for food poisoning – the incidence of which has been rising steadily in Britain
- Food processing further separates the urban consumer from the farm. Many children do not know how food is grown or how animals are reared
- Between 1978 and 1998, the distance food was transported increased by 50%
- Transporting animals long distances to slaughter has made it almost impossible to contain outbreaks of serious diseases such as foot and mouth
- Journeys of 200-400 miles to slaughter are not unusual for animals today
- The average journey to abattoir has been estimated at 100 miles
- In 1996, Britain imported 233,000 tonnes of beef – 80,000 tonnes of which were from outside the EU. The beef came from as far away as Namibia (9,500km) and Australia (21,000km)
- In order to be transported long distances food must be heavily processed, packaged, or chemically preserved
- 25m tonnes of waste was produced in Britain in 1997 and one-third of that was packaging
- Britain's food market is dominated by five big supermarket groups: Tesco, Sainsbury's, Asda, Safeway and Somerfield
- The big five between them account for more than 80% of all grocery sales
- The combined profits of the top four supermarkets were £2.1bn in 2000

- An inquiry by the competition commission looked into whether cheaper farm prices were passed on to the consumer. It found that the fall in prices which has hit farmers was passed on to the consumer – or that where it was not, this was because there were other increases elsewhere in the supply chain
- The inquiry also found that the real price of food had fallen by more than 9% between 1989 and 1998
- Supermarket profits are much greater than the combined income of all UK small farmers
- Each new major supermarket in a city has been found to cause up to 200 job losses
- The food we eat is increasingly processed
- Sales of chilled ready meals grew by 12% in 1999, while fresh fruit consumption fell by 3%, although sales of fresh fruit and vegetables had been increasing
- The major growth area in 1999 was in processed meats and meat products. Frozen convenience meat products have grown by 127% since 1978
- **Milk**. Farmers get an average of 17p a litre for milk, though it costs them an average of 22p a litre to produce. A typical supermarket price is 35p a litre
- **Beef**. It is almost impossible for a farmer to make a living producing beef in this country. Compensation for BSE cost £607 million
- **Fruit**. We now import four out of every five pears we eat. 65% of apple orchards have been lost. We imported 434,000 tonnes of apples in 1996. Cox's receive an average of 16 pesticide sprays
- **Salad**. Lettuces can come from Spain, Turkey, Zimbabwe and Mexico. A typical crop will be sprayed 11.7 times

© Guardian Newspapers Limited 2001

It's a burger of a problem

In Britain we eat more burgers than anyone else in Europe – burger restaurants are our favourite high street eating places. But do we really know exactly what we're getting? Perhaps not . . .

What's your beef?

The law says burgers can be called '100% beef' even if they contain up to 15% water and up to 35% extra fat. Supermarket beefburgers are labelled, but they can contain water, soya and milk protein, colourings, flavouring, seasoning and sugar as well as various chemicals.

Antibiotic overload

Some beef comes from intensive or factory farms where large numbers of cattle are raised in sheds. Crowding makes them more prone to disease, so they are routinely fed antibiotics.

Antibiotics are also used to boost animal growth. Cattle are fed similar antibiotics to the ones we are given when we have serious illnesses. And now there's evidence that those illnesses are becoming resistant to antibiotics as a result. This reduces our own ability to fight disease.

Lettuce eat our greens

More pesticides are applied to lettuce than any other field crop – an average of 12 different treatments per year. In 1998, nine out of ten UK lettuces had traces of pesticides. Tomatoes are grown in heated greenhouses that encourage diseases – so they get treated with pesticides too.

Bad deal at the meat market

UK beef prices have fallen, spelling a tough time for our farmers. Like the cocoa growers in the developing world, they're struggling to get a fair price for their produce. Yet the price of beef products sold to consumers in the shops has not gone down. Are the big food companies really giving farmers a fair deal?

Grass is greener

There can be other chemicals in meat, too: grass and other cattle feed is treated with chemical fertilisers and pesticides. And that's bad news for wildlife on farms and for our water, as well as for our burgers. There are now worries that cattle are being fed genetically modified (GM) soya feed: meat produced in this way doesn't have to carry a label saying so.

GM-free?

The oil that your burger and fries are cooked with can come from soya. But much of the soya imported to the UK is already harvested from genetically modified (GM) plants. GM technology is still poorly understood and it could have serious long-term effects on the environment and our health. Some burger chains say they're GM-free – but it's always best to check.

Veggie alert

Veggie burgers are often made from various soya products – so check that they don't include GM soya.

What the burger chains say on GM

McDonald's say that all their burgers are free of GM ingredients. However they are still working towards finding GM-free derivatives (e.g. oils or lecithin that have come from GM soya or GM maize). (June 1999)

Burger King says that it is taking steps to remove GM ingredients from its products but currently cannot guarantee that the soya and maize in any of its products – including the buns and oil – is GM-free. (May 1999)

© Friends of the Earth

Understanding food labels

Information from the Ministry of Agriculture, Fisheries and Food (MAFF)

Two fruit drinks might claim 'high juice', and cost about the same. But the labels may show that one contains twice as much juice as the other. Food labels must give information so that we can choose between foods.

Even if we don't want to read everything on labels, the law controls what they say, to protect us from false claims or misleading descriptions.

There are rules for words and pictures. For instance, a food label isn't allowed to boast 'reduced calorie' unless the product inside really is much lower in calories than the ordinary version. A yoghurt can't show strawberries on the pot unless the flavour comes mainly from strawberries.

Are you convinced that it's good sense and good housekeeping to use food labels?

Reading labels can give us:
• Value for money
As well as comparing pack weights, we can use the ingredients list on labels to choose which product we want.

• A taste we're looking for
If we like our ice-cream to contain milk fat, we can look for the one labelled 'dairy', only allowed on products made with milk fat.

• Freedom to avoid ingredients we don't want or shouldn't eat
Labels list ingredients, including additives and added water.

• The facts behind claims
If a label makes a claim like 'extra fruit', it also has to back it up by showing the minimum amount of fruit.

• Help in avoiding food poisoning
Most perishable foods have to show a 'Use by' date, and give instructions for safe storage.

• Help in preparation.

• Facts about healthy eating
More and more products label the amount of calories, fat, sugars, fibre and salt in them.

• Information on where food comes from.

What's in a name?
When is bacon vegetarian? When it's a crisp! Smoky bacon *flavour* crisps and chicken *flavour* crisps need contain no bacon, chicken or other meat. Just as the name says, they have a flavour of them.

The laws that the name of a product must not be misleading.

Whenever the name of a food contains the word 'flavour', the food doesn't have to contain any of that ingredient, but a food labelled 'Cheese and onion pasty' must contain cheese and onion.

The most important job of a food label is to tell us clearly what the food is. Saying 'paté' isn't enough, because there are many kinds. So the label, or a notice on the shop shelf, must say what sort of paté it is.

The name also has to tell us if the food has undergone any type of process, such as UHT milk, smoked mackerel, dried apricots.

Pictures must not mislead. A yoghurt that gets its raspberry flavour from artificial flavouring, not completely or mainly from fruit, isn't allowed to have a picture of raspberries on the pot.

But what about cream crackers? A few well-known foods are allowed

to keep the names we all know them by, because we're not likely to be misled. We know that cream crackers don't contain cream, that white grapes aren't really white and that Swiss rolls don't have to come from Switzerland.

But if something we expect to come from one place – such as Cornish clotted cream – isn't made there, the label must state where it is made.

What is it made of?
Labels on most packed foods must list all the ingredients. The list can tell us a lot about a food – and whether it's what we want.

Value for money
Ingredients, including additives, are listed in descending order of weight at the time of their use in the preparation of the food. So if we buy mushroom soup, we get more mushrooms than other ingredients where mushrooms come nearest the top of the ingredient list.

The list does not have to give the amounts of any ingredient. But a fruit yoghurt that lists sugar higher than fruit probably has only a small amount of fruit in it, no matter how pink it looks.

We may not mind if a food contains less of more expensive ingredients if we like the taste and the price is right. But without the ingredients list, we would not know what we were choosing.

If a food label makes a special claim such as 'with extra chocolate', then the label must show the minimum amount of that ingredient. We can decide for ourselves whether we think the product is worth our money.

Additives
Most food additives have to be included in the ingredients list. The food company must show the name of each additive, or its 'E' number, or both. Before each name, the label

says what sort of additive it is, for instance 'Preservative'.

Labels help us decide for ourselves

For flavourings, labels must either say if they have been used or give their names.

Some people read food labels just to avoid all additives. But it's more practical to judge each sort separately. For instance, many of us accept preservatives so we can keep food longer without spoiling, yet prefer food without colouring. Others are happy provided colourings come from natural sources. Others like the brightness colours can add to food.

Unwrapped food

Food that is sold unwrapped – such as some bread, food from a cooked food counter and sweets – doesn't carry an ingredients list. But a ticket or notice nearby must show its proper name, and the type of any main additives in it, such as 'contains preservative'.

Labelling to avoid food poisoning

Datemarking

It's easy to see when an apple is going rotten. But food poisoning wouldn't be a problem if we could always tell that food was 'off' by smelling or looking at it.

The dates marked on food labels are an important safeguard against food which may be unfit to eat – or just unpleasant. They help all of us to maintain food safety and quality. They also help us to identify and use safely both highly perishable foods and foods with a longer shelf-life.

'Use by'

The 'Use by' datemark is for highly perishable foods which could become a food safety risk, such as some meat products or ready-prepared meals.

It is not always obvious when food has become unsafe to eat.

'Use by' is a clear instruction – we should use the food by the end of the date given on the label. Using food beyond this date could put our health at risk. We should not rely on our senses alone to tell us when food is 'off'. It is not always obvious when

food has become unsafe to eat. However, 'Use by' does not necessarily mean 'eat by' because cooking or freezing food before its 'Use by' date can extend its life.

What about 'Best before'?

Most food that can safely be kept longer carries a 'Best before' datemark. When that date runs out, it doesn't mean that the food may be dangerous. But it may no longer be at its best. Even frozen, dried and canned foods start to deteriorate in the end.

So if we want to enjoy the food at its best, we should use it by its 'Best before' date.

What to look for

Manufacturers must put the datemark in a prominent place on the label. The date will normally be alongside the words 'Best before' or 'Use by' but, if this is difficult, the manufacturer must tell us where to find the date, for example 'Best before: see date on lid'.

Other instructions

There is a lot we can all do to keep our food safe from the time we buy it to the time we eat it. Label information can protect our health by giving storage and preparation instructions.

'Use by' and 'Best before' dates are based on us following storage instructions properly. If we don't, food will spoil more quickly, and we may risk food poisoning.

Manufacturers may also provide further instructions, such as 'Best on day of purchase' or 'Eat within 3 days of opening', which we should follow.

Some retailers mark food with 'Display until' dates, but these are instructions to shop staff rather than us.

Make sure the fridge or freezer is cold enough. Aim to keep the coldest part of the fridge between 0°C and 5°C and the freezer below minus 18°C. Use a thermometer to check.

Directions for preparing food can also protect us against illness. Recommended defrosting and cooking times are tested by food companies to cook food at a temperature that kills any harmful bacteria (such as salmonella), as well as producing tasty results.

Food with no datemark

A few foods do not have to carry a datemark. Some, such as fresh fruit, vegetables and some cakes, are normally bought for use within a very short period and it is clear when their quality is deteriorating. Food that is not pre-packed, such as meat bought from a butchers, is also unlikely to carry a datemark. Others, such as alcoholic drinks, sugar, salt and vinegar last for such a long time that a datemark is unnecessary. However, it is a good idea to mark long-life foods with the date we bought them so that we can use the oldest first.

The law

The law requires most food to carry a datemark. These dates cannot be changed by unauthorised persons. Food labels carrying 'Use by' dates must be withdrawn from sale once that date has passed. If you are worried about a particular datemark, consult the shop-keeper or manager. If you are still not satisfied, contact the Trading Standards Department or the Environmental Health Department of your county, district or borough council.

Remember

- Check datemarks in the shop and at home. Use earliest dates first.
- Always eat products before the end of their 'Use by' date, or cook or freeze for later use.
- Check and follow storage instructions.
- Follow any additional instructions, for example 'Eat within two days of opening'.
- And if in doubt – throw it out!

© Ministry of Agriculture, Fisheries and Food (MAFF)

Labels without a cause

Mary-Vere Parr wonders if new 'assurance' schemes will really help farmers or consumers

When the National Farmers' Union launched its British Farm Standard last June, hopes were high that here, at last, was a logo that could boost flagging UK farming fortunes. Slapped on 100 fresh product lines, from red meat to fruit and veg, in supermarkets throughout the country, the BFS red tractor, promised the NFU, would help UK farm produce stand out against the piles of foreign food.

At present, we import £2.6 billion worth of produce that could be grown or reared in this country.

Something more than patriotism was at play here. In the wake of BSE, consumers are concerned to know how – and where – their food is produced. And they say that they want to buy British meat on quality and animal welfare grounds.

The problem is that the plethora of 'farm assurance' labels fails to provide meaningful information on production methods. Even the label 'British' is questionable, because it can be applied to goods produced elsewhere but packaged or processed in this country.

The NFU's red tractor logo was supposed to provide the ultimate reassurance. 'The British Farm Standard is a promise to consumers that all foods carrying the little red and blue tractor logo have been produced to the highest possible standards of food safety, animal welfare and environmental care,' the NFU's president, Ben Gill, declared.

But what does it really mean? Existing farm assurance schemes – such as Farm Assured British Beef and Lamb, Quality Meat Scotland and Farm Assured Welsh Livestock – automatically meet the British Farm Standard, which is in effect an umbrella scheme designed to simplify red tape for producers. These schemes ensure that farmers comply with legal requirements, such as health and safety, and meet Government animal welfare guidelines. However, the recommendations are general and cover intensive farming as well as organic.

There is also confusion over whether the mark really denotes British produce. Consumers could be forgiven for thinking that buying products bearing the red, white and blue logo meant buying British. However, under EU rules, foreign producers can join the scheme, as long as they meet UK production criteria. The confusion has prompted a complaint to the Advertising Standards Agency by the independent consumer watchdog, the Food Commission, London.

The problem is that the plethora of 'farm assurance' labels fails to provide meaningful information on production methods

---

Nevertheless, the scheme has scored some success. Each week,

Tesco sells 3,000 tonnes of British chicken, beef, lamb and pork; and this autumn it will extend its red tractor lines as more British fruit and veg comes into season. But the red tractor will be hard pushed to rival Tesco's organic range, sales of which have doubled year on year over the past three years.

Although Professor John Krebs, head of the Food Standards Agency, has questioned the accreditation of the imported food that makes up 80 per cent of the UK organics market, it seems that consumers believe that an organic label is the only one that offers genuine farm assurance. Post-BSE, they prefer to trust the Soil Association, the main UK certifying body for organic produce, rather than the Government's Food Standards Agency.

The future lies in schemes that offer traceability – the ability to track food back to individual farms and specific production methods – says Tim Lobstein, co-director of the Food Commission, London. 'It's not only important that consumers can do a full tracking of food but inevitable, as product liability is extended to food,' he says. Under EU legislation, from December 4, every farmer will in theory be liable for the food he or she produces, in the way that manufacturers are liable for faulty goods.

In these circumstances, the solid red tractor with its chunky blue wheels looks a little broad-brush. Indeed, six months on from its endorsement at a Downing Street farming summit in March, staff at the Blairs' former local Sainsbury's in Islington were unable to explain what the logo meant.

Undaunted, this autumn the NFU ran a 'trusty farmer' competition to kickstart the campaign. Look out for posters of fresh-faced farmers selling their wares in a supermarket near you.

© *Telegraph Group Limited, London 2000*

Europe sees Britain as home of tainted food

By Andrew Osborn

The UK's reputation as a meat producer – already stained by BSE – is looking positively tainted after this week's outbreak of foot-and-mouth disease. As Andrew Osborn reports from Brussels, European consumers will be even more reluctant to buy British.

For Europe's already traumatised army of consumers the outbreak of foot-and-mouth disease in the UK will confirm what they have suspected all along – that Britain is a country where the food tastes bad and is tainted by disease.

It doesn't matter that foot-and-mouth cannot be passed to humans via infected meat like mad cow disease for in the minds of consumers perception and fear is everything.

Britain, for many on the continent, is rapidly acquiring a reputation as a country which acts as an incubator for some of the world's nastiest animal diseases, and its agricultural credentials have now hit rock bottom.

As if to illustrate the point a brave band of souls from the British Meat and Livestock Commission were in France this week for its annual agricultural fair.

But they had made the mistake of taking a few sheep along with them to liven up their stand and swiftly found themselves in the embarrassing situation of having to test the animals for foot-and-mouth disease antibodies. Distrust of the UK's already battered farming industry is at an all-time low.

First there was BSE, which is now spreading across Europe leaving a trail of fear and paranoia in its wake, and then last summer Britain's pigs were struck down by swine fever forcing the European Commission to slap an export ban on the UK which was only lifted after thousands of animals had been slaughtered.

European consumers have been reading about export bans on British meat products for the past five years and the outbreak of foot-and-mouth disease could be the final nail in the coffin. Dangerous, tainted and diseased are words which, rightly or wrongly, are increasingly associated with British food products and it could take years to dispel the many myths and misunderstandings which live on in people's minds.

The UK may have chosen to unilaterally impose its own export ban on animal products after it discovered foot-and-mouth in Essex but the government also has to contend with an EU-wide export ban from Brussels and many European countries will need firm assurances before they agree to lift it.

When the EU's food safety spokeswoman briefed the international press corps on the issue earlier this week she was faced with a barrage of alarmist questions from journalists all over the world demanding cast-iron assurances that Britain's problems will not become their problems.

'Can it affect humans?' asked one Italian journalist. The answer – 'not really' – obviously failed to satisfy many and when the EC admitted that there was a tiny risk of viral infection through close contact between infected animals and older people, children and pregnant women, the alarm bells began to ring. 'Can you catch it by drinking milk?' asked another and so it went on.

One of Britain's most lucrative export markets for animal products – the EU itself – is at stake and the government and the UK farming industry must do everything they can to reassure our European partners that the outbreak is under control.

If it does turn out that the source of the infection lies beyond Britain's shores it will undoubtedly be a useful tool in persuading our trading partners that there is nothing endemically tainted about UK food production techniques.

But the nightmare scenario, and one which the government must be dreading, is that the highly contagious disease will be carried on the wind, on the soles of tourists' shoes or on the wheels of cars, to continental Europe.

If that happened it would be hard to imagine how Britain could ever hope to rebuild its export markets for meat. The challenge facing Britain's beleaguered farmers is tough enough as it is already.

Food poisoning 'hits over 8 million a year'

By Sean Poulter, Consumer Affairs Correspondent

A hidden food poisoning epidemic is sweeping Britain, with as many as 8.3 million cases each year, according to a damning study by Government watchdogs.

The Food Standards Agency says the real scale of the problem is far greater than official figures suggest, and it has demanded hygiene improvements.

Some 14 per cent of people surveyed by the FSA said they have had food poisoning in the past year, showing signs of vomiting and diarrhoea.

If the pattern were repeated across the UK population of 59.5 million, the total number of victims would be 8.3 million.

These figures are over 80 per cent higher than those official FSA estimates, which suggest there are up to 4.5 million cases of food poisoning a year.

The watchdog has set itself a target of reducing cases by 20 per cent over the next five years, which will involve a major clean-up of fast food outlets, butchers, supermarkets and in the home.

A massive 78 per cent of those surveyed said they were fairly or very concerned about food safety. The safety of handling raw meat was a particular worry for 69 per cent.

Less than half – 48 per cent – were confident about current food safety measures, which is a reflection of scandals running from BSE to salmonella in chicken and eggs, and E.coli.

The FSA chairman, Sir John Krebs, said: 'Less than half of consumers are confident about current food safety measures. It may be a reflection of two decades of food crises but it is an unacceptably low level.

'This survey reveals the food issues that matter most to consumers. It highlights consumer concerns on food poisoning and BSE. The responsibility for change rests with everyone involved in the food business.'

He said the FSA was earning the trust of the public and it would 'continue to champion measures to improve food safety and consumer confidence'.

> **Some 14 per cent of people surveyed by the FSA said they have had food poisoning in the past year**

A summary of the FSA's findings makes clear that few people bother to report the problem and simply retire to bed, costing the economy some £743 million a year in lost working hours and medical treatment.

The figures give some backing to the suggestion that people build up a tolerance to food poisoning bugs over time.

Only 3 per cent of those over 66 reported falling ill, compared with 20 per cent of those aged 26-35.

The relatively high number of victims in their late twenties and early thirties could also be because this group is most likely to eat out.

Other elements of the survey suggest there is much confusion about the healthy eating messages coming from the Government.

The FSA said: 'Comprehension of what was a significant level of fat, sugar and, in particular, salt, was variable and general understanding of ingredient labelling was poor.'

Just 36 per cent of respondents knew that they should be eating five portions of fruit and vegetables a day for a healthy diet.

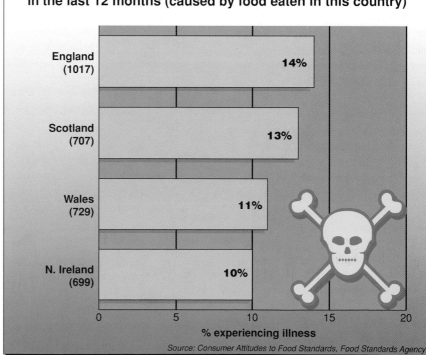

Food poisoning

Respondents were asked of any experience of food poisoning in the last 12 months (caused by food eaten in this country)

- England (1017): 14%
- Scotland (707): 13%
- Wales (729): 11%
- N. Ireland (699): 10%

% experiencing illness

Source: Consumer Attitudes to Food Standards, Food Standards Agency

Despite concerns about BSE and food poisoning, we are still very much a nation of meat eaters, with only one in 20 UK households including a vegetarian. Some 90 per cent eat fresh meat, with chicken being the favourite. The study is based on a survey of 3,153 people across the UK.

The campylobacter bug is now the biggest single source of food poisoning in the UK.

Surveys by the FSA have found that more than nine in ten fresh and frozen chickens are contaminated with campylobacter, and 94.5 per cent of the 13 million pigs slaughtered in the UK in the past year tested positive for the bug.

Campylobacter is associated with the normal signs of food poisoning, including upset stomach and loss of fluids, which can be extremely serious for the elderly, sick, young or mothers-to-be.

In a few cases, it can cause life-threatening secondary illnesses such as Guillain-Barre syndrome which brings on total temporary paralysis.

Bugs 'found in 16% of supermarket chicken'

By Felicity Lawrence

Food poisoning bugs are rife in chickens, with almost one in six bought from supermarkets a potential food risk, according to a report from the Consumers' Association.

A survey published today in *Which?* magazine says that tests on more than 300 fresh raw chickens and chicken pieces found 16% containing unwelcome bacteria, including salmonella. The tests used are not the most sensitive and may well underestimate the scale of the problem.

Which? went undercover to a slaughterhouse to investigate the causes, and found live chickens in crates stacked on top of each other.

'These crates were made of plastic mesh with spaces large enough for faeces to drop through on to the birds below and spread bacteria. After being killed the birds were dunked in a scalding tank to make their feathers easier to remove. The water was changed only once a day. Many thousands of dead chickens went through it. Brown scum floated on the top – the water was cool enough for salmonella and campylobacter [the commonest form of food poisoning bacteria] to live in.'

The magazine said that in the area where birds were cut into pieces, staff were handling chickens without cleaning their gloves. 'Our source told us he had seen a member of staff return to his job still wearing an apron which had trailed in a urinal when he visited the lavatory. Chickens left over after the firm had sent out the day's orders were rewrapped the next day with a new sell-by date,' a practice which a Meat Hygiene Service source said he feared went on at other slaughter-houses. 'Chickens aren't born with salmonella or campylobacter, they catch it,' the association said. 'This can happen at any stage in the food chain. On the farm infection can spread if chickens are confined in small spaces.'

In the *Which?* tests, chicken from Tesco was found to be contaminated the least, in 6% of cases. Sainsbury's, at 22%, and Safeway, at 21%, were the worst.

The wrapper that can tell whether your snack is safe

By James Chapman

A plastic wrapper that can detect when food inside is not safe to eat has been developed by scientists.

It changes colour if it comes into contact with salmonella, E. coli and other food poisoning bugs, thanks to a coating of antibodies.

The Canadian firm behind the breakthrough, Toxin Alert of Toronto, says the wrapper can also be adapted to detect pesticides and genetically-modified ingredients.

Vice president Gord Furzer told the *New Scientist* magazine it would cost about 25 per cent more than normal plastic film but believes it will prove popular with food manufacturers who want to reassure customers, and people who want to keep leftovers at home.

'If you can afford a sandwich bag you should be able to afford one of our sandwich bags,' he said. Mr Furzer admitted the product would not pick up low levels of bacteria that can still cause illness. 'What we're looking at is stopping gross contamination that causes mass illness and death,' he said.

But an American expert, microbiologist Mike Doyle of Georgia University, said: 'They are going to give people a false sense of security. There are a lot of disease-positive products out there that are not going to get picked up.'

Hygiene ratings may be displayed in eating places

By James Meikle

Britain's 550,000 eating places and food shops – from top hotels to hospital canteens and burger vans – might have to display hygiene scores to help customers choose whether to use them.

The ratings would be based on inspections by local council officials on compliance with health, safety, and food handling regulations.

The government's food standards agency is discussing the idea with consumer groups and environmental health bodies. Enthusiasts say scores would increase consumer power, and point to a US system of publishing information on food hygiene arrangements on visiting cruise ships as a model. This is said strongly to influence tourist bookings.

Food standards officials believe a system for publishing individual ratings could be added to new arrangements for local authority reporting of food poisoning incidents and hygiene standards within their areas.

These will mirror tougher inspection regimes and league tables already introduced by the government for schools and social services, and reflect government concern at the patchy nature of food hygiene enforcement.

They will be phased in from January if they are approved by the agency's board later this month. In addition, all food businesses will soon have to prove themselves worthy of holding licences to trade under EU rules which will take four years to introduce. The Consumers' Association yesterday called on the public to help to combat the huge under-reporting of food poisoning cases. Only about 100,000 a year are formally recorded and it is believed the true figure could be 4.5m in England alone. As many as 60 people a year may die.

Ann Goodwin, of the Chartered Institute of Environmental Health, which is also involved in the discussions on hygiene scores, said: 'Why not inform consumers? Then they can vote with their feet.'

> **All food businesses will soon have to prove themselves worthy of holding licences to trade under EU rules which will take four years to introduce**

She said there was no reason why a voluntary scheme could not be introduced quickly once a national framework was agreed, even if formal regulation might take longer. 'What would businesses have to hide?'

The agency is already planning big increases in information local councils have to provide so it can compare the performance of different types of shops, restaurants and other food outlets in different areas, even if these would not be individually named at present. These tables will be published and agency officials will also inspect councils' environmental health departments and demand improvements where necessary.

Tom Murray, head of the agency's local authority enforcement division, confirmed the publication of individual ratings was being considered carefully but there were difficulties to overcome. 'Any system we put together would have to be objective and robust and applied consistently.'

Businesses might just be having a bad day when inspected. Should new owners or managers have to display poor ratings from previous management? Such arrangements could not be put in place over a couple of months when there were so many food businesses, in more than 500 local authorities.

Proper food storage in the refrigerator

Information from the European Food Information Council (EUFIC)

Refrigerator storage is an important way of keeping food safe. The cool temperature helps to keep the food fresh and slow the growth of most harmful microbes. At the same time, it does not change the characteristics of the food.

The proper temperature for a refrigerator is 5°C on the middle shelf. However, the temperature is not constant throughout the interior. By taking advantage of the temperature differences, you can ensure optimal storage for all your food.

The coldest point in the refrigerator is the bottom shelf on the drawers used for vegetables (2°C). This is the place to put fresh meat and fish. Placing them at the bottom also prevents them from dripping onto other foods.

Store eggs, dairy products, sandwich meats, leftovers, cakes, and products marked 'Refrigerate when opened' on the middle shelves (4-5°) and the top shelf (8°C). The drawers at the bottom (up to 10°C) are intended for vegetables and fruits that can be damaged by lower temperatures. The compartments or shelves on the inside of the door are the warmest part of the refrigerator (10-15°C) and are intended for products that need only light refrigeration. These include drinks, mustard and butter.

Do not put too much food in the refrigerator. If it is loaded to the point that there is no space between the items, air cannot circulate and this affects the temperature distribution. If frost is allowed to accumulate, the refrigerator will not function efficiently. In addition space is reduced when frost builds up. Defrost your refrigerator regularly using warm water with a little bit of vinegar to remove odours.

Note that some foods do not need, and may even lose quality, by refrigeration; for example, exotic fruits, tomatoes, green beans, cucumbers and zucchini. Bread goes stale more quickly in the refrigerator. Fruits and vegetables that need to ripen should also be kept at room temperature.

During summer, the temperature dial will need to be set at a colder setting than during the winter. Be sure the door is closed tightly at all times. Open the doors only when necessary and close them as soon as possible.

Wrap or cover food to prevent loss of moisture and flavour. Put leftovers in clean, shallow covered containers. Do not put large amounts of warm food in the refrigerator as this will raise the temperature; cool the food for a short time at room temperature (remember that any cooked leftovers should be put into the refrigerator within two hours after being served).

Practice FIFO (First-In-First-Out). When stocking food storage areas, place recently purchased items behind items that are already there. This procedure will help ensure that you are consuming food prior to expiration date/spoilage and helps reduce the amount of food that has to be discarded.

Keep in mind that food is kept safe in the fridge only as long as indicated on the label. If you have doubts about a food, or about how long it has been in the refrigerator, throw it out. A great help is also a fridge thermometer to make sure that the refrigerator is always at a safe temperature.

If you have doubts about a food, or about how long it has been in the refrigerator, throw it out

• The above information is an extract from *Food Today*, published by EUFIC. See page 41 for address details.

© European Food Information Council (EUFIC)

A few more bugs in our food and we'd be healthier

'Last week research revealed that a third of children under four are overweight. Sterile convenience meals are to blame'

Catherine Pepinster interviews Anthony Worrall Thompson

When I was a child I used to spend a lot of time with my grandmother, who cooked me wonderful meals. Those were the days when we weren't so obsessed with hygiene and germs. It was normal to take in milk bottles with silver tops pecked by the birds, and store food in the larder. We didn't think every item of food should be kept in the fridge – if we had a fridge – or think that it was a disaster for meat to be placed next to other foodstuffs.

My grandmother often used to make trifle, and one Sunday I told her that the trifle did not taste the same as usual. She dipped her finger in the red sauce adorning the top of the pudding – and discovered that it was blood which had dripped onto the trifle from a roast rib of beef. I was none the worse for it; I didn't suffer an upset stomach (in those days we didn't have food poisoning, we had upset stomachs).

I am not an advocate of sloppiness in the kitchen, or unhygienic practices, but we have gone too far in our pursuit of germ-free food. Despite all our endeavours to improve hygiene, all that seems to have happened is that the outbreaks of food poisoning have increased. I believe that some of the problem is caused by the obsession we have about cleanliness. We used to develop natural defences so that our bodies could tolerate more, but today we don't build up our immune systems. Our obsession with bacteria could be the death of us.

There are other, hidden dangers from food. The amount of fats, sugars and salts in processed food, for instance, is undoubtedly harmful. Only last week researchers from Liverpool University revealed that almost a third of children under four are overweight, including nearly one in 10 who are classified as obese. The study blamed parents' reliance on ready meals, with high fat content, for the increase in children's weight, and warned that it will lead to heart disease and other health problems.

A hundred years ago, 4lbs of sugar per person per year were consumed; today that figure has risen to 160lbs

We should be more discerning: not all fats are bad for us. Olive oil is a good healthy alternative to animal fat. And in our concern about saturated fats we have ignored the amount of 'transfats' we eat. These ingredients – man-made, processed substances such as margarine – are particularly harmful and are linked to health problems. It's not as if the food industry does not know how harmful they are. As long ago as 1956, the *Lancet* carried a study which showed that hydrogenation in food manufacture could contribute to various diseases such as cancer. And in the US, an experiment was carried out using cockroaches. Cockroaches usually eat anything but when some margarine was put in a cage, none of them would touch it.

I believe other health problems are caused by ingredients in our food: the chemicals added during factory processing, the antibiotics which animals are given, which could be passed on to us. All contribute to lowering our immune systems. There are theories that the increasing number of allergies – and the high incidence of asthma in children – is caused by pollution. I'm not so sure. I grew up when there were pea-souper fogs and factories belching fumes, yet the incidence of chest problems among children seemed far less. I can't remember anyone experiencing

an anaphylactic shock after eating a peanut, or being stung by a wasp.

Then there is our high sugar intake. A hundred years ago, 4lbs of sugar per person per year were consumed; today that figure has risen to 160lbs. No wonder we have seen the incidence of diabetes increase 10-fold in the past 40 years.

Juice junkies probably think fruit is far better for them than manufactured fizzy drinks. But they forget that juice contains sugar in the form of fructose. It's the same with medicine.

There are people who believe that a carbohydrate rich diet is a healthy diet. They read that it is wise to eat plenty of pasta and brown bread. But they forget that kind of diet suits an athlete. If you eat lots of carbohydrate and don't take plenty of exercise, it turns to glucose, which turns to fat.

It is important we are well informed about the origins and processing of food. The consumer should know what he or she is eating

– and especially what children are eating.

Even better would be to go organic. For some people, that is not a realistic option because much organic food is unaffordable. Specialist shops charge high prices, although some supermarkets have a good range, and are not so costly. But as more of us demand organic produce and the supply increases, so prices should come down. A word of warning. There's no point buying organic produce if it's been flown in – wasting energy – when home-grown produce is better in terms of

both taste and the impact on the environment. My tip: back local food. Or even better, grow your own.

People who do grow their own know the other secret of food: it's not that hard to cook delicious meals. Nor does it take long. I remember the time when I went to a motorway café and asked for a plain omelette. I could have a mushroom one, or a ham one, but plain? No. Why not? They bought them frozen, and it took three minutes to cook. If they'd started from scratch, it would have taken one-and-a-half minutes to make.

The best food is fresh, tasty and simple. It's a myth that cooking it is difficult and time-consuming. If we believe that, we end up with the food we deserve.

• Antony Worrall Thompson is a chef. He was speaking yesterday at the 'We are what we eat . . . But who decides?' conference in London.

© The Independent Newspaper Ltd
11th February, 2001

Should we be afraid to eat?

Information from the European Food Information Council (EUFIC)

Eating is now perceived to be a dangerous business. As more and more news about food scares hits the headlines, we feel that the list of foods that could make us sick gets longer. Public health statistics show a rise in food-borne diseases caused by micro-organisms. We are also told that these diseases are under-reported.

Should we be afraid to eat? In Europe, food is plentiful and of good quality. Thanks to science, technology and strict regulation, it is mostly safe. Why are we so worried? One reason is that food issues are important to us and stories of food-borne illness provoke an emotional response — everyone has to eat. Governments, science and industry are often criticised in their failure to address consumers' fears rapidly and convincingly. The media, on the other hand, may stretch facts to make a catchy story.

Another reason for public anxiety is that improved communications allow news, especially bad news, to travel widely and quickly. Thanks to the media attention to food-borne disease, consumers are becoming aware of microbiological risks in food. This leads to increased reporting. 'Stomach upsets' that once would have gone unnoticed are now reported as cases of food poisoning.

Certainly, food-borne illnesses caused by micro-organisms are a real challenge. Micro-organisms are a

natural part of our world and the only way to reduce them is to take special measures throughout the food chain and during storage and preparation at home. A failure in the food supply chain affects many people because of the potential scale of the operations. Incidents of this type usually make the headlines. However, many food-borne infections or intoxications can be traced to poor hygienic practices in the home.

Lifestyles are changing. Many modern consumers are too busy to spend time in the kitchen. They may have forgotten the basic rules about food hygiene and yet they still expect their food to be safe. Unfortunately, most foods naturally contain some microbes and raw foods may contain pathogens. Compounding this problem is the fact that many foods that have been developed to meet consumer demands for convenience and freshness (for example, chilled foods) need careful handling throughout the distribution chain and at home.

Consumers are changing. As life expectancy increases, the number of immuno-compromised and elderly people grows. They are especially susceptible to food-borne illness.

This does not mean that food is less safe today. Despite wide public perception and frequent media coverage that our food safety is declining, the food we buy today has never been safer and we should not be afraid to enjoy it. However, we take safe food for granted and sometimes forget our role in safe food handling at home.

Consumer information and education about the active role we play in safe food handling are key strategic elements for keeping pace with changing times and technologies.
• The above information is from the European Food Information Council (EUFIC). See page 41 for address details.

School dinners link to infected pigs

By Felicity Lawrence, Consumer Affairs Correspondent

The search for the source of the foot-and-mouth epidemic switched to pig swill made from the leftovers from schools and restaurants yesterday.

Robert Waugh, the Northumberland farmer whose pigs are thought to have been the source of the outbreak, said they had been fed on swill made from waste collected from schools in Sunderland and Gateshead.

Sunderland city council confirmed that it had had a contract with Mr Waugh's brother Ronnie to collect school waste for free, but the contract had been terminated in January when he asked for money for taking it away.

Gateshead council said that it had an informal arrangement for the collection of 'plated waste' from their schools. The Waughs also used waste from local restaurants.

Robert Waugh was licensed by the Ministry of Agriculture to feed the waste to his pigs and says that it was heat-treated as required by law.

Heating should inactivate foot-and-mouth, according to Stephen Curry, a researcher in the biophysics department at Imperial College, London.

But there has been anecdotal evidence of meat products being the cause of the disease in the past. Mr Waugh's suggestion that he had not fed his pigs 'anything that hadn't already been served up on bairns' plates' caused alarm among parents.

Although humans cannot catch foot-and-mouth from eating meat, and the source cannot yet be confirmed, it raised the possibility that the school meals had contained infected meat.

All large catering companies use burgers, sausages, mince and other cheap processed meats in their cooking, and the quality depends on the cost specified in their contracts with schools.

'There have been so many problems around meat that people do now distrust school meals,' said Joe Harvey, director of the Health Education Trust.

New standards for school meals will be enforced from April.

But processed meat is often made from inferior quality materials.

Mechanically recovered meat (MRM), a slurry produced from pig and chicken bones, is still used. The regulations permit the use of the rectum, testicles, udders, feet and tails in MRM for cooked meat products.

Because of BSE, MRM may no longer be made from the vertebral columns of ruminants in the EU, but the rules do not apply to meat products imported from outside the EU.

It is an offence to import meat products from a country which has foot-and-mouth.

ADDITIONAL RESOURCES

You might like to contact the following organisations for further information. Due to the increasing cost of postage, many organisations cannot respond to enquiries unless they receive a stamped, addressed envelope.

British Nutrition Foundation (BNF)
High Holborn House
52-54 High Holborn
London, WC1V 6RQ
Tel: 020 7404 6504
Fax: 020 7404 6747
E-mail: british/
nutrition@compuserve.com.
Web site: www.nutrition.org.uk
The (BNF) is an independent charity which provides reliable information and advice on nutrition and related health matters. They produce a wide range of leaflets, briefing papers and books. Ask for their publications list.

European Food Information Council (EUFIC)
1 Place des Pyramides 75001
Paris
France
Tel: + 33 140 20 44 40
Fax: + 33 140 20 44 41
E-mail: eufic@eufic.org
Web site: www.eufic.org
EUFIC is a non-profit making organisation based in Paris. It has been established to provide science-based information on foods and food-related topics, i.e. nutrition and health, food safety and quality, and biotechnology in food for the attention of European consumers. It publishes regular newsletters, leaflets, reviews, case studies and other background information on food issues.

Food Standards Agency
Aviation House
125 Kingsway
London , WC2B 6NH
Tel: 020 7276 8000
Web site:
www.foodstandards.gov.uk
The UK Food Standards Agency is a new organisation established by Act of Parliament. The Agency has been created to 'protect public health from risks which may arise in connection with the consumption of food, and otherwise to protect the interests of consumers in relation to food'. Runs the Food Standards Agency Helpline on 0845 757 3012.

Friends of the Earth (FOE)
26-28 Underwood Street
London, N1 7JQ
Tel: 020 7490 1555
Fax: 020 7490 0881
E-mail: info@foe.co.uk
Web site: www.foe.co.uk
As an independent environmental group, Friends of the Earth publishes a comprehensive range of leaflets, books and in-depth briefings and reports.

Institute of Food Research
External Relations Office
Norwich Research Park
Colney
Norwich, NR4 7UA
Tel: 01603 255000
Fax: 01603 255168
Web site: www.ifr.bbsrc.ac.uk
The Institute of Food Research is a UK centre for research of international quality, sponsored by the Biotechnology and Biological Sciences Research Council. Their mission is to carry out independent research on food safety, quality, nutrition and health.

Ministry of Agriculture, Fisheries and Food (MAFF)
Nobel House
17 Smith Square
London, SW1P 3JR
Tel: 020 7238 3000
Fax: 020 7238 6591
Web site: www.maff.gov.uk/
maffhome.htm
MAFF has four policy aims. The aims are broad and contain a number of objectives within each of them. The aims are: to protect the public, to protect and enhance the rural and marine environment, to improve the economic performance of the agriculture, fishing and food industries and to protect farm animals. The MAFF Helpline is a local call rate number (0645 33 55 77 within the UK) available between 09.00 and 17.00 on working days.

The Soil Association
Bristol House
40-56 Victoria Street
Bristol, BS1 6BY
Tel: 0117 929 0661
Fax: 0117 925 2504
E-mail: info@soilassociation.org
Web site: www.soilassociation.org
Works to educate the general public about organic agriculture, gardening and food, and their benefits for both human health and the environment.

INDEX

★★★★★

The Internet has been likened to shopping in a supermarket without aisles. The press of a button on a Web browser can bring up thousands of sites but working your way through them to find what you want can involve long and frustrating on-line searches.

And unfortunately many sites contain inaccurate, misleading or heavily biased information. Our researchers have therefore undertaken an extensive analysis to bring you a selection of quality Web site addresses.

British Nutrition Foundation (BNF)
www.nutrition.org.uk
A very comprehensive web site covering such topics as nutrition facts, nutrition news and education. Well worth a visit.

Food Standards Agency
www.foodstandards.gov.uk
The Food Safety Information Bulletin and the Food Surveillance Information Sheets, which have comprehensive food information, can be viewed with ease on this useful web site.

Friends of the Earth (FOE)
www.foe.co.uk
By clicking on Real Food you will find the latest information and press releases on a wide range of food-related issues. Lots of briefings etc.

Institute of Food Research
www.ifr.bbsrc.ac.uk
An excellent web site. Sometimes very technical but generally good. For easy to read food facts click on Food Information Sheets

Ministry of Agriculture, Fisheries and Food (MAFF)
www.maff.gov.uk/maffhome.htm
Click on Food and Drink or do a search for documents, which cover a wide range of food and drink safety issues.

The Soil Association
www.soilassociation.org
For a long list of topics, press releases and publications click on the Library button. Then go to Briefing Papers. Here you will find a range of articles which outline the views of the Soil Association on GM issues. The GMO link is also worth a look.

ACKNOWLEDGEMENTS

The publisher is grateful for permission to reproduce the following material.

While every care has been taken to trace and acknowledge copyright, the publisher tenders its apology for any accidental infringement or where copyright has proved untraceable. The publisher would be pleased to come to a suitable arrangement in any such case with the rightful owner.

Chapter One: The Food We Eat

Enjoy healthy eating, © Crown copyright is reproduced with the permission of the Controller of Her Majesty's Stationery Office, *Fat in food*, © Crown copyright is reproduced with the permission of the Controller of Her Majesty's Stationery Office, *Guidelines for a healthier diet*, © Institute of Food Research, *The plate of the nation*, © The Co-operative Group, *The real diet of the nation*, © The Co-operative Group, *School children*, © British Nutrition Foundation, *Burger battles*, © Guardian Newspapers Limited 2000, *Government launches free fruit in schools*, © Crown copyright is reproduced with the permission of the Controller of Her Majesty's Stationery Office, *Ban the junk food ads*, © The Daily Mail, July 2000, *Food adverts*, © The Daily Mail, July 2000, *The rich get thin, the poor get fat*, © Telegraph Group Limited, London 2000, *Health drive targets beer and fast food lifestyle*, © Guardian Newspapers Limited 2000, *Diet and weight*, © 2001 Mosby International Limited, *Eating habits*, © Crown copyright is reproduced with the permission of the Controller of Her Majesty's Stationery Office, *Report on obesity*, © British Nutrition Foundation, *Organic farming*, © The Soil Association, *Are organic foods healthier than the alternatives?*, © Guardian Newspapers Limited 2000, *Organic foods 'not more nutritious'*, © Guardian Newspapers Limited 2000, *Soil Association responds to Food Standards Agency*, © Soil Association, *Antibiotics in food*, © Soil Association.

Chapter Two: Food Safety

A general introduction to food safety, © Institute of Food Research, *Low public trust in food safety*, © Guardian Newspapers Limited 2000, *Consumer attitudes to food standards*, © Crown copyright is reproduced with the permission of the Controller of Her Majesty's Stationery Office, *Top ten facts and figures*, © Crown copyright is reproduced with the permission of the Controller of Her Majesty's Stationery Office, *Concerns about food issues*, © Crown copyright is reproduced with the permission of the Controller of Her Majesty's Stationery Office, *Tackling BSE*, © New Scientist, RBI Limited 2001, *From farm to plate*, © Guardian Newspapers Limited 2000, *It's a burger of a problem*, © Friends of the Earth, *Understanding food labels*, © Crown copyright is reproduced with the permission of the Controller of Her Majesty's Stationery Office, *Labels without a cause*, © Telegraph Group Limited, London 2000, *Europe sees Britain as home of tainted food*, © Guardian Newspapers Limited 2001, *Food poisoning 'hits over 8 million a year'*, © The Daily Mail, February 2001, *Food poisoning*, © Crown copyright is reproduced with the permission of the Controller of Her Majesty's Stationery Office, *Bugs 'found in 16% of supermarket chicken'*, © Guardian Newspapers Limited 2000, *The wrapper that can tell whether your snack is safe*, © The Daily Mail, April 2000, *Hygiene ratings may be displayed in eating places*, © Guardian Newspapers Limited 2000, *Proper food storage in the refrigerator*, © European Food Information Council (EUFIC), *A few more bugs in our food and we'd be healthier*, © The Independent Newspaper Ltd, 11th February, 2001 *Should we be afraid to eat?*, © European Food Information Council (EUFIC), *School dinners link to infected pigs*, © Guardian Newspapers Limited 2001.

Photographs and illustrations:

Pages 1, 6, 7, 18, 28, 37: Pumpkin House, pages 3, 9, 15, 20, 27, 33, 36, 38, 40: Simon Kneebone

Craig Donnellan
Cambridge
April, 2001